Cambridge Primary

Revise for Cambridge Primary Checkpoint

Practical revision activities
to prepare learners for the
Cambridge Primary Checkpoint test

English
Teacher's Guide

Stephanie Austwick

Series editor: Kate Ruttle

HODDER
EDUCATION
AN HACHETTE UK COMPANY

The Publishers would like to thank the following for permission to reproduce copyright material:

Acknowledgements
Terry Nation: text extract from *Rebecca's World* (Red Fox, n/e, 1986), p51; **Beverley Naidoo:** text extract from *Journey to Jo'burg* (HarperCollins Children's Books, 2008), p53; **Michael Morpurgo:** text extract from *Running Wild* (HarperCollins Children's Books, 2009), pp55 & 109; **Frank Linderman:** 'The Bark of a Birch Tree' from *Indian Why Stories*, found on www.native-languages.org/blackfootstory3.htm (originally published by Charles Scribner's Sons, 1915), p57; **Ian Serraillier:** 'Mountains' from *The Sun Goes Free, and other poems* (Longman, 1977), © Estate of Ian Serraillier, by permission of Jane Serraillier, p59; **Nigel File and Chris Power:** 'Francis Barber' from *Black Settlers in Britain* (Heinemann Educational Books, 1982), pp76 & 78; **Philip Pullman:** text extract from *Spring-Heeled Jack* (Corgi Yearling, Second edition, 1998), copyright © 1989 by Philip Pullman, p85; **Rhoda Nottridge:** text extracts from *Cartoons (Films)* (Hodder Wayland, 1992), p96; **Wikipedia:** 'How films are made', web page from http://en.wikipedia.org/wiki/Filmmaking, p98.

Extracts adapted with permission of Louis Fidge and Brenda Stones.

Every effort has been made to trace all copyright holders, but if any have been inadvertently overlooked the Publishers will be pleased to make the necessary arrangements at the first opportunity.

Although every effort has been made to ensure that website addresses are correct at time of going to press, Hodder Education cannot be held responsible for the content of any website mentioned in this book. It is sometimes possible to find a relocated web page by typing in the address of the home page for a website in the URL window of your browser. Websites included in this text have not been reviewed as part of the Cambridge endorsement process.

Hachette UK's policy is to use papers that are natural, renewable and recyclable products and made from wood grown in sustainable forests. The logging and manufacturing processes are expected to conform to the environmental regulations of the country of origin.

Orders: please contact Bookpoint Ltd, 130 Milton Park, Abingdon, Oxon OX14 4SB. Telephone: (44) 01235 827720. Fax: (44) 01235 400454. Lines are open 9.00–5.00, Monday to Saturday, with a 24-hour message answering service. Visit our website at www.hoddereducation.com.

© Stephanie Austwick 2013
First published in 2013 by
Hodder Education,
An Hachette UK Company
Carmelite House, 50 Victoria Embankment,
London EC4Y 0DZ

Impression number   5 4 3
Year   2017 2016

Cover illustration by Peter Lubach
Illustrations by Planman Technologies
Typeset in ITC Stone Serif Medium 10/12.5 by Planman Technologies
Printed in Great Britain by CPI Group (UK) Ltd, Croydon, CR0 4YY.

A catalogue record for this title is available from the British Library.

ISBN: 978 1444 178319

Contents

Introduction

About the series

The *Revise for Cambridge Primary Checkpoint* series is designed to provide teachers and learners with resources to support preparation for the Cambridge Primary Checkpoint tests in English, Mathematics and Science.

The Cambridge Primary curriculum

The Cambridge Primary curriculum provides schools with an appropriate and internationally relevant framework to develop the learners' skills, knowledge and understanding in the key areas of English, Mathematics and Science. The curriculum frameworks set out detailed learning objectives for each year of primary education from Stage 1 to Stage 6 to provide clear progression and expectations of what the learners will achieve by the end of each stage.

Cambridge Primary Checkpoint

To enable assessment of achievement in each subject area, the Cambridge Primary curriculum frameworks are supported by internationally benchmarked tests called Cambridge Primary Checkpoint. These diagnostic tests are designed to help teachers track the learners' performance, identify specific strengths and weaknesses, and provide progress reports for the learners and their parents. The tests focus on assessing knowledge and understanding of the learning objectives for Stages 4, 5 and 6 and include multiple-choice and matching activities, and short- and long-answer questions.

The *Revise for Cambridge Primary Checkpoint* series provides focused revision activities for all strands of the frameworks examined in the Cambridge Primary Checkpoint tests. The **Teacher's Guide** enables easy planning of revision lessons around particular areas of need. The learners can extend their revision independently using the activities and challenges in the **Study Guide**. There is a variety of assessment opportunities across the series. These include informal quizzes and Checkpoint-style practice papers, to enable teachers and learners to identify gaps in knowledge and support areas that require additional practice.

> On photocopiable pages with this symbol 📖, the learners will require extra paper.

Ways to use this book

This **Teacher's Guide** is divided into four chapters: 'Phonics, spelling and vocabulary', 'Grammar and punctuation', 'Reading' and 'Writing' to match the Cambridge Primary *English Curriculum Framework*. It also includes practice tests, which can be used to revisit the content of the previous chapters and prepare learners for the Cambridge Primary Checkpoint test.

Each chapter is divided into strands with a page of teacher's notes, containing information and ideas for revision, and a photocopiable page of activities to support the learning. The revision activities include model texts, questions and investigations as well as fun games to make and play. These pages could be used within the lesson or as independent or homework activities. Answers to these activities can be found at www.hoddereducation.com/cambridgeextras.

The photocopiable 'quick quizzes' at the end of each chapter draw together various aspects of the strands and offer teachers an opportunity to assess understanding and give the learners a taster of the style of questions found in the Cambridge Primary Checkpoint tests.

The activities in the **Study Guide** are directly related to the strands in the **Teacher's Guide** and may be used to further support and extend the revision prior to the test, either in the classroom or on an independent level.

Syllabus coverage

Used in conjunction with the accompanying **Study Guide**, the revision activities in the **Teacher's Guide** cover all the learning objectives that will be assessed in the Cambridge Primary Checkpoint English test. The Speaking and Listening objectives (4SL1–4SL8, 5SL1–5SL11, 6SL1–6SL10) are not covered explicitly as they are not assessed in the Cambridge Primary Checkpoint test. It is assumed that all learning objectives will have been covered in depth during prior teaching of the curriculum. For this reason, some minor learning objectives are not covered in great detail and skills-based objectives are often found in practice opportunities throughout the revision lessons. For example, in the 'Top tips' sections, teachers are encouraged to remind the learners to practise skills such as reading more widely, reviewing and editing their written work, presenting their written work appropriately.

Objectives overview

The following chart shows where the objectives from the *English Curriculum Framework* are covered within the **Teacher's Guide** and **Study Guide**. Each Framework code identifies a unique objective in the curriculum framework using the stage number, strand, sub-strand (where applicable) and bullet number. For example, 4PSV1 references Stage 4, Phonics, spelling and vocabulary strand, bullet one: 'Extend knowledge and use of spelling patterns, e.g. vowel phonemes, double consonants, silent letters, common prefixes and suffixes'. A complete list of the framework objectives and codes can be found at www.hoddereducation.com/cambridgeextras.

Chapter	Strand	Framework codes	Teacher's Guide page numbers	Study Guide page numbers
Phonics, spelling and vocabulary	Vowel and consonant phonemes	4PSV1 4PSV3 5PSV5 6PSV3	6–7	6–7
	Common letter strings	4PSV5 4PSV11 5PSV2 6PSV3	8–9	8–9
	Spelling rules	4PSV4 4PSV6 4PSV7 5PSV1 5PSV4 5PSV6 5PSV7 6PSV4	10–11	10–11
	Prefixes and suffixes	4PSV8 5PSV7 5PSV9 5PSV10 6PSV6	12–13	12–13
	Synonyms and antonyms	4PSV12 4PSV13 4PSV14 5PSV15 5PSV16 6PSV8	14–15	14–15
	Homophones	4PSV9 5PSV3 5PSV11 6PSV3	16–17	16–17
	Plurals	4PSV7 5PSV1 5PSV8 6PSV3 6PSV4	18–19	18–19
Grammar and punctuation	Nouns and pronouns	5PSV3 5GPw6 6GPr2	24–25	22–23
	Verbs	4PSV2 4GPr6 4GPw3 5GPr3 6GPr6	26–27	24–25
	Adverbs and adjectives	4GPr5 5PSV14 6GPr2 6Wf7	28–29	26–27
	Prepositions	5GPr2 6GPr2	30–31	28–29
	Compound sentences	4GPw4 5GPw5 5GPr5 6GPr4	32–33	30–31
	Complex sentences	4GPw4 5GPw4 6PSV7 6GPr3 6GPr8 6GPw2 6GPw4 6GPw5	34–35	32–33
	Commas	4GPr4 5GPw1 6GPw5	36–37	34–35
	Apostrophes	4GPr3 5GPw2 6GPw1	38–39	36–37
	Direct and reported speech	4GPw2 4GPw3 5GPr1 5GPr4 5GPw3 6GPw1	40–41	38–39
	Using a range of punctuation	4GPr1 4GPr2 4GPw1 4GPw5 6GPr1	42–43	40–41
Reading	Historical stories – settings	4Rf3 5PSV13 5Rf1 6Rf2	48–49	44–45
	Fantasy stories – characters	4Rf4 5Rf8 6Rf2 6Rf3	50–51	46–47
	Stories from other cultures – inference and atmosphere	4Rf1 4Rf9 5Rf1 5Rf2 5Rf6 6Rf3 6Rf11	52–53	48–49
	Stories with issues – authors and viewpoints	4Rf4 5Rf7 6Rf1 6Rf2 6Rf9	54–55	50–51
	Fables, myths and legends – the parts of a story	4Rf6 4Rf7 5Rf9 6Rf4	56–57	52–53
	Poetry – figurative language	4Rf5 4Rf13 5Rf4 5Rf5 5Rf6 5Rf12 6PSV11 6Rf7	58–59	54–55
	Play-scripts	4Rf9 4Rf12 5Rf11 6Rf5 6Rf11	60–61	56–57
	Autobiographies and biographies	5Rn6 6Rn3	62–63	58–61
	Persuasion	4Rn5 5Rn5 5Rn9 6Rn1 6Wf3 6Wn6	64–65	62–63
	Discussion	4Rn1 5Rf10 5Rn8 6GPw3 6Rn4 6Wn7	66–67	64–65
	Instructions	4GPr7 4Rn3 5Rn8 6Rn2	68–69	66–67
	Explanations	4Rn2 5Rn7 6Rn5	70–71	68–69
	Recounts	4Rn3 4Rn4 5Rn6 6Rn2	72–73	70–71
	Reports	4Rn3 5Rn1 6Rn2	74–75	72–73
Writing	Planning stories	4Wf1 5Wf1 6Wf1	80–81	78–79
	Openings and endings	4Wf4 5Wf4 6Wf2 6Wf7	82–83	80–81
	Settings and characters	4Wf3 5Wf8 6Wf1 6Wf4	84–85	82–83
	Adding detail	4PSV12 4PSV14 4Wf2 4Wf7 5Wn3 6Wf7	86–87	84–85
	Organisation and paragraphing	4Wf6 5Wf6 6GPw2 6Wf5 6Wf6	88–89	86–87
	Audience and purpose	4Wn2 6Wn2	90–91	88–89

Phonics, spelling and vocabulary

Vowel and consonant phonemes

Learning objectives

- Extend knowledge and use of spelling patterns and apply phonic / spelling knowledge when reading unfamiliar words. (4PSV1, 4PSV3)
- Use effective strategies for learning new spellings and misspelt words and apply patterns to improve accuracy. (5PSV5, 6PSV3)

Let's revise!

- Revise the difference between the pronunciation of long and short vowels and remind learners of the different ways of making the most common long vowel phonemes (see the chart on photocopiable page 7).

- When teaching phonics, it is important to start with speaking and listening. To orally revise a chosen long vowel phoneme, play the *Nonsense rhyming game* as a class. First, display and read a simple nonsense rhyme like the one below, and discuss the use of the long *oo* phoneme:

  > There was a teacher whose name was *Sue*
  > She liked to think of good things to *do*
  > So, one day she took her class to the *zoo*
  > They didn't stay long, just had a walk *through*
  > They saw lots of animals, not just a *few*

- Next, ask the learners to decide on a long vowel phoneme, and collaboratively make up a rhyme. Point out that the rhyme doesn't have to make sense! Write the learners' ideas on the board. For example, the following rhyme is based around the long *ee* phoneme:

  > One day I fell over and injured my knee
  > And when I got home, I'd forgotten my *key*
  > So, I got in a boat and I sailed out to *sea*

  Make a list of the rhyming words used in the class rhyme and discuss the spelling of the phonemes.

- Ask the learners to write their own nonsense rhymes in pairs, taking extra care with spelling. Encourage the learners to focus on the long vowel sounds in their rhymes and ask them to compile a list of the words containing their chosen vowel phoneme.

- Challenge the learners to choose a long vowel phoneme, make a list of words containing this phoneme, then write a mini story of less than 100 words, using as many words from the list as possible. See the example on photocopiable page 7.

Top tips

Build up interactive displays on the wall. Investigate the different ways of spelling the long vowel phonemes and arrange the words in 'families', putting together all the words that have the same spelling of the phoneme, for example: few, new, knew, chew; rude, tune; spoon, moon, food. Encourage the learners to investigate the spelling of these phonemes and add to the display whenever possible.

Study Guide

See pages 6–7 of the Study Guide for further long vowel phoneme revision.

Name: _____

Long vowel phonemes

Long *a*		Long *e*		Long *i*		Long *o*		Long *u*	
ay	day	**e**	be	**i**	find	**o**	no	**u**	use
a–e	game	**ee**	deep	**i–e**	hide	**ow**	crow	**o**	to
ai	pain	**ea**	stream	**igh**	light	**oe**	toe	**oo**	food
eigh	eight	**y**	funny	**y**	by	**oa**	road	**ew**	blew
ea	great	**i**	piano	**eye**	eye	**o–e**	note	**ough**	through
ei	reindeer	**ie**	thief						
		ei	ceiling						

1 Look at the different ways of spelling the long vowel phonemes. Tick (✓) the ones you think are the most common.

2 Draw a line between the words that have the same long vowel phonemes. The first one has been done for you.

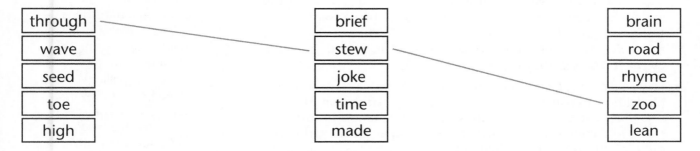

through	brief		brain
wave	stew		road
seed	joke		rhyme
toe	time		zoo
high	made		lean

Mini story phoneme spotter

3 Circle the words with the long *o* vowel phonemes. Can you find 33 words?

> Long ago there was a lonely toad who lived in a hole not far from the lake. So, he decided to go and to visit Mole, who lived over the other side of the road.
>
> 'I'm so lonely,' he croaked. 'I don't know what to do.'
>
> 'Oh dear,' replied his friend. 'Why don't you go and row around the whole lake? You will meet lots of toads, voles, moles and stoats. When you go home you will have so many new friends.'
>
> So, Toad rowed over the boating lake and made so many friends he was never alone again.

Phonics, spelling and vocabulary

Common letter strings

Learning objectives

- Spell words with common letter strings but different pronunciations, e.g. *tough, through, trough, plough.* (4PSV5)
- Check and correct spellings and identify words that need to be learned. (4PSV11)
- Recognise a range of less common letter strings in words which may be pronounced differently. (5PSV2)
- Continue to learn words, apply patterns and improve accuracy in spelling. (6PSV3)

Let's revise!

- A common letter pattern or 'string' is a sequence of letters that occurs frequently. Ask the learners to think of some letter strings and make a general revision list. Some will be prefixes and suffixes, such as *pre-* and *-tion*, whereas some will be strings such as *tch, dge, ough, ight* and *str*. Make class lists that can be added to by the learners as they discover new words.

- Play *Letter string tennis* to revise common letter patterns in words. Model how to play with a partner. Choose a string from the class lists that have been made. With your partner, take it in turns to say a word containing this string. For example, for the string *ight*: sight, night, light, bright, fight, etc. Try to avoid hesitation or repetition.

- Revise the fact that although some letter strings rhyme, others are pronounced differently. For example, for the string *ough* there are several pronunciations: rough, cough, through, thorough.

- Ask the learners to complete the task on photocopiable page 9 of grouping words according to pronunciation. It is important to say these words out loud and clarify meanings where necessary.

- Ask the learners to play *Spot and spell* to consolidate the different pronunciations of the common letter patterns and their meanings. Put the learners into pairs labelled A and B. Ask Learner A to make up a sentence containing one of the words in the *ough* list from photocopiable page 9, for example: 'The clever dolphin jumped through the hoop.' Learner B then writes down the *ough* word, ensuring the correct spelling, and shows Learner A. Learner A checks the spelling, they swap roles and repeat. This game can be used to revise any list of words or groups of spellings.

Top tips

- Learning about common letter strings can help the learners to make informed choices when faced with unknown spellings. Sometimes, however, unusual or irregular words (such as *enough* and *through*) need to be seen, written, investigated and used on a regular basis for them to become internalised.

- Making and playing word games is a great way of seeing these words over and over again. Use *Letter string lotto* on photocopiable page 9 to revise some of these words.

Study Guide

Pages 8–9 of the Study Guide encourage learners to revise other common letter strings.

Name: _____

Common letter strings

A letter pattern or 'string' is a sequence of letters that is often found in words. Some letter strings, such as *ough,* are spelt the same but can be pronounced differently.

| tough | trough | enough | cough | thought | rough |
| bough | dough | plough | ought | although | bought |

1 Some of the words in the box above rhyme. Group them according to pronunciation and write them in the table below.

1.	2.	3.	4.	5.
tough				
enough				
rough				

2 Can you add any more words to the lists above?

3 Can you think of some *ough* words that don't even fit into these lists?

_____

_____

4 Can you create any rules that might help with pronunciation? For example, what happens if *ough* is followed by a *t*? Is this letter string always pronounced in the same way?

Letter strings lotto

Make your own *Letter strings lotto* game to play with your friends.

1 Make some lotto cards, dividing each one into nine sections.

2 Decide on six common letter strings and write them into the boxes of the lotto card. Make each card different by repeating different strings.

3 Make lists of words that contain the strings and write each word on smaller pieces of card.

4 The caller turns over a word card, reads the word and players who have that letter string on their card cover the box with a counter. They can only cover one box at a time.

5 The first person to cover all nine boxes is the winner. Have fun!

str	tion	igh
ough	ear	wh
igh	str	ear

Phonics, spelling and vocabulary

Spelling rules

Learning objectives

- Identify syllabic patterns in multisyllabic words. (4PSV4)
- Investigate spelling patterns; generate and test rules that govern them. (4PSV6)
- Revise rules for spelling words with common inflections, e.g. *-ing, -ed, -s.* (4PSV7)
- Investigate the spelling of word-final unstressed vowels, e.g. the unstressed 'er' at the end of butter and unstressed 'ee' at the end of city. (5PSV1)
- Identify 'silent' vowels in polysyllabic words, e.g. *library, interest.* (5PSV4)
- Learn spelling rules for words ending in *-e* and *-y*, e.g. *take / taking.* (5PSV6)
- Know rules for doubling consonants and investigate patterns in the use of single and double consonants, e.g. *-full / -ful.* (5PSV7)
- Further investigate spelling rules and exceptions, including representing unstressed vowels. (6PSV4)

Let's revise!

- Revise the spelling rules to help the learners to work out the spelling of new words. For example, look at the rule used when changing the form of the verb and adding *-ing*:
  - Drop the *-e* and add *-ing* (chase – chasing, write – writing, take – taking).
- Give the learners one minute to write down as many examples of this rule as they can. They should write the original verb followed by the new form. Orally rehearse some of these in a sentence if appropriate.
- Try the same activity with a different spelling rule, such as when changing a noun to an adjective:
  - Drop the *-e* before adding the *-y* (ice – icy, breeze – breezy, shade – shady).
- Ask the learners to create spelling rules for adding *-ed, -er* or *-est* to a word ending in *-e*, for example: shape – shaped, care – carer, close – closest. Some learners will prefer to keep the pattern of the rules above, as it has a rhythm to it, for example: drop the *-e* and add *-ed*; others will make up their own rules, for example: just add the *-d*, you don't need another *-e*! The most important thing is that they realise that rules are there to help them remember how to spell new or unfamiliar words.
- Ask the learners to revise words with unstressed vowels using the activities on photocopiable page 11.

Top tips

- Spelling rules with a rhythm or a rhyme tend to stick in the mind more easily. If the rule is too complicated it doesn't really help the learner and is often forgotten.
- It is a good idea to ask the learners to carry out their own investigations and create their own rules.
- Encourage the learners to keep a record of words with unstressed vowels in a book as tricky words to remember.

Study Guide

See pages 10–11 of the Study Guide for more spelling investigations and some exceptions.

Name: _____

Spelling rules

Some words contain vowels that many people do not say out loud or pronounce in a quick or different way. These are called unstressed vowels.

> For example:
> business   is often pronounced 'biz-ness' and not 'bizz-i-ness'
> description   is often pronounced 'diss-crip-tion' and not 'dee-scrip-tion'
> separate   is often pronounced 'sepp-ret' and not 'sep-ar-ate'

1   Sound out the syllables in each of the following words as if you are beating a drum. Then write each word out in syllables and underline the vowels.

conference   con-fer-ence

deafening   _____

general   _____

miserable   _____

difference   _____

2   What do you notice about each syllable?

    _____

    _____

3   Read these words aloud then say them in a sentence, as you would normally pronounce them. Underline the vowel that is unstressed when you say each word aloud.

    secretary   jewellery   ordinary   stationery   library

4   What do you notice about the endings of each of the words above
    (for example secret**ary**)?

    _____

    _____

    _____

5   Find three other words that contain unstressed vowels.

    a _____

    b _____

    c _____

Phonics, spelling and vocabulary

Prefixes and suffixes

Let's revise!

- Revise the use of prefixes and suffixes:
  - **prefix:** a group of letters that goes in front of a root word; prefixes change the meanings of words, for example: patient – impatient
  - **suffix:** a group of letters that can be added to the end of a root word to change its meaning or the way in which it is used.
- A suffix can make a new word in one of two ways:
  - **inflectional** (grammatical): for example changing singular to plural: boy – boys; past tense to present: walked – walking; the basic meaning of the word does not change; these are sometimes referred to as inflections, and you may decide to teach them separately
  - **derivational** (the new word has a new meaning or word class, derived from the root word): for example verb changes to a noun: teach – teacher; noun or verb changes to an adjective: care – careful.
- Make a list of common prefixes (such as *re-*, *pre-*, *un-*, *dis-*, *de-*, *im-*) and discuss their meaning. Place a number of root words on cards. Ask the learners to take a card from the pile and add a prefix to the word. Ask the learners what the prefix does to the meaning of the root word.
- Often the prefix creates the opposite of the root word. Play *Fortunately / Unfortunately* to revise ways of creating opposites. Set the scene for a story, for example:

  Once upon a time, there was a young man called Samir who loved to travel the world. He wanted to visit as many countries as possible, so one day he set off for the airport.

  Ask the learners to take it in turns to add a sentence, starting with 'Fortunately' or 'Unfortunately', for example:

  Unfortunately, when he got there, there were very long queues at the check-in desks.

  Fortunately, he decided to fly to the North Pole and there was no queue at all.

- As a class, make a list of common suffixes, for example: *-acy*, *-al*, *-ance*, *-er*, *-or*, *-dom*, *-ity*, *-ness*, *-ship*, *-ify*, *-able*, *-sion*, *-tion*, *-ist*, *-ism*, and discuss how these change the root words.
- Hide these lists and ask the learners to put as many prefixes and suffixes as they can into the boxes on photocopiable page 13.
- Ask the learners, in pairs, to find as many words as they can where a root word has to be modified before the suffix can be added, for example beaut**y** – beaut**i**ful, or the final consonant must be doubled before the suffix is added, as in jo**g** – jo**gg**ing – jo**gg**er. Challenge them to create rules to explain these processes to the class.

Name: _____

Prefixes and suffixes

1 Add as many prefixes and suffixes as you can to the table.

Common prefixes	Common suffixes

2 Read about Pip. He is the sort of brother most people would like to have.

Pip was a rather <u>kind</u> and <u>considerate</u> boy.

One day, he had to leave the house before his brother, Ricky, got back from school.

<u>Fortunately</u>, on this occasion, Pip had been very <u>responsible</u>. He had been <u>careful</u> and had left the back door <u>unlocked</u>.

It was quite <u>thoughtful</u> of him as it would mean that it would be <u>possible</u> for Ricky to get inside and get on with his homework.

When Ricky arrived he was very <u>pleased</u> when he tried the door. Because of Pip's <u>unselfishness</u>, Ricky's homework would be <u>finished</u>.

3 Now try changing Pip completely! Add or remove prefixes or suffixes to give the underlined words the opposite meaning.
For example, if the text says 'possible', replace it with 'impossible';
if it says 'careful', replace it with 'careless'.

Read through what you have written and check that it makes sense.

Phonics, spelling and vocabulary

Synonyms and antonyms

Learning objectives

- Use more powerful verbs, e.g. *rushed* instead of *went*. (4PSV12)
- Explore degrees of intensity in adjectives, e.g. *cold*, *tepid*, *warm*, *hot*. (4PSV13)
- Look for alternatives for overused words and expressions. (4PSV14)
- Use a thesaurus to extend vocabulary and choice of words. (5PSV15)
- Collect synonyms and opposites and investigate shades of meaning. (5PSV16)
- Explore definitions and shades of meaning and use new words in context. (6PSV8)

Let's revise!

- Revise the following definitions:
  - **synonyms:** words that have **s**imilar meanings (make the connection between **s** and **s**)
  - **antonyms:** words that have opposite meanings (*anti* = 'opposite').
- Focus on synonyms, pointing out that these can be:
  - verbs – talk, chatter
  - adverbs – happily, merrily
  - adjectives – quickly, swiftly.
- Prepare some lists of adjectives that are synonyms. You could use a thesaurus. For example:
  - angry, furious, mad, fuming, annoyed
  - hungry, famished, starving, ravenous
  - tired, exhausted, worn-out, weary.

  Write these words onto cards – one word on each card – and give them out. Ask the learners to find the rest of their adjective 'family' and sit in a group. Discuss the words in each 'family'. Ask each group to stand in order of intensity. For example, is 'exhausted' more tired than 'weary'? (Remember that the meanings are only *similar*.)

- Play *Synonym drama*. Ask the learners to explore a verb by listing synonyms for the word and then acting them out to experience what they look and feel like. For example, for 'walk', they might act out trudge, saunter, stroll and totter.

- Then play *Antonym drama*. The learners must act out an adverb and its antonym. For example, they might walk happily and miserably, or confidently and nervously. Ask the learners to contribute adverbs and their opposites.

- Ask the learners, in pairs, to use a thesaurus to generate some interesting lists of synonyms. They should then put these words into a sentence and discuss which sentence sounds best.

- Give each learner photocopiable page 15. After they have completed the activities, listen to some of the versions of 'Dolly' and discuss their word choices, focusing on verbs, adverbs and adjectives, and on strong, unusual or descriptive words.

Top tips

Remind the learners that, when they are writing, it is important to explore synonyms in order to choose the best word, with the correct intensity, and avoid repetition.

Study Guide

See pages 14–15 of the Study Guide for further revision on synonyms and antonyms.

Synonyms and antonyms

Synonym = similar meaning   **Antonym = opposite meaning**

1 Match the three synonyms with one antonym. Look up any words you are unsure of.

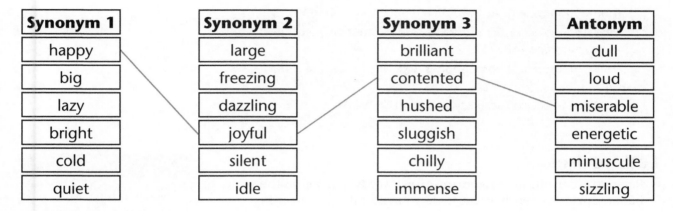

Synonym 1	Synonym 2	Synonym 3	Antonym
happy	large	brilliant	dull
big	freezing	contented	loud
lazy	dazzling	hushed	miserable
bright	joyful	sluggish	energetic
cold	silent	chilly	minuscule
quiet	idle	immense	sizzling

Meet Molly and Dolly!

Molly and Dolly were twins.

Molly was a very cheerful girl. On her way to school, she would smile at everyone she met. When she arrived in the playground, she would call out a cheerful 'Hello' to the other children and everyone was pleased to see her.

The teachers said that they had never known such a polite, hard-working girl and that she was a pleasure to have in the class.

Because of her wonderful behaviour, she had so many friends and life for Molly was always happy.

But Dolly! What a difference. She was just the opposite!

2 Using antonyms, write a passage to describe Dolly, beginning with:

On the other hand, Dolly was a very miserable girl.
On her way to school, she would … 🗒

Phonics, spelling and vocabulary

Homophones

Learning objectives

- Match spelling to meaning when words sound the same (homophones), e.g. *to / two / too, right / write*. (4PSV9)
- Spell and make correct use of possessive pronouns, e.g. *their, theirs, my, mine*. (5PSV3)
- Revise grammatical homophones, e.g. *they're, their* and *there*. (5PSV11)
- Continue to develop accuracy in spelling. (6PSV3)

Let's revise!

- Revise the definition of **homophones:** words that sound the same but are spelt differently because they have a different meaning.
- Revise a few common homophones and discuss their meanings, for example: their / they're / there; to / two / too; sea / see; hear / here; new / knew; be / bee; wear / where.
- Ask the learners to complete the sentences on photocopiable page 17, then work in pairs to generate a list of homophones and record them in the box on the page. Discuss their lists and ways of remembering them. For example:
  - **there:** has the word 'here' in it – here and there
  - **they're:** is short for 'they are' and nothing else
  - **their:** belongs to – their house.
- Explore how making up silly sayings or rhymes can help the learners to remember which one is which. These are called mnemonics. For example:
  - their / there / they're: This one **belongs to E**gor, **I**gor and all **R** friends.
  - here / hear: You h**ear** with your **ear**.
  - beech / beach: The b**ea**ch is next to the **sea** but a b**ee**ch is a tr**ee**.
  - threw / through: Th**rew** is the past tense of th**row**.
- Invite the learners to make up their own mnemonics for homophones they find particularly tricky to remember. They could try adding actions and teach these to each other. For example:
  I can **hear** you driving in your c**ar**
  With an h and an e and an r and an e, I'm over **here** for all to see.

Top tips

- Many learners find the spelling of similar words difficult to remember, so regular practice is essential. Ask the learners to write the words they find hard three times. First in pencil, then in crayon, then in an interesting way, such as in rainbow colours, in bubble writing, backwards, as small as possible, with the other hand, and so on.
- Remind the learners that mnemonics can often be helpful, particularly if there is a rhythm, an action or even an illustration.

Study Guide

See pages 16–17 of the Study Guide for some homophone writing activities.

Name: _____

Homophones

Homophones are words that sound the same but are spelt differently.

1 Fill in the correct homophones.

some / sum	The farmer could only find _____ of his sheep.
right / write	Don't forget to _____ a thank you letter to your aunt.
to / too / two	I'm sorry but this soup is much _____ spicy for me.
whole / hole	I've just written a _____ page about my holiday.
great / grate **beach / beech**	The boy was having a _____ time on the _____.

2 How many other pairs, or groups, of homophones can you think of?

3 Make up ways of remembering the ones you find confusing, for example:

To do s**um**s you need to know all your n**um**bers (not just **some** of them)!

Phonics, spelling and vocabulary

Plurals

Learning objectives

- Revise rules for spelling words with common inflections, e.g. *-ing, -ed, -s*. (4PSV7)
- Investigate the spelling of word-final unstressed vowels, e.g. the unstressed 'er' at the end of butter and unstressed 'ee' at the end of city. (5PSV1)
- Investigate spelling patterns for pluralisation, e.g. *-s, -es, -y / -ies, -f / -ves*. (5PSV8)
- Continue to learn words, apply patterns and improve accuracy in spelling by further investigating spelling rules and exceptions, including representing unstressed vowels. (6PSV3, 6PSV4)

Let's revise!

- Revise the four main (regular) rules for pluralisation:
  1 For most nouns, just add *-s*, for example: book – books.
  2 For nouns that end in *-ss, -sh, -ch* or *-x*, you need to add *-es* to help you say the word, for example: box – boxes, brush – brushes.
  3 For some nouns that end in *-y*, you change the *-y* to an *i* and add *-es*, for example: fly – flies.
  But … if there is a vowel before the *-y*, you just add *-s*, for example: key – keys.
  4 For nouns that end in single *-f* or *-fe*, you *usually* change the ending to *-ves*, for example: half – halves.

- To assess the learners' knowledge, call out a mixed selection of nouns with regular plurals and ask the learners to write them down and then hold them up for you to see. You could use: cat, box, shelf, wish, monkey, door, jelly, cow, leaf, match, car, fox. It is important to say the singular version so that learners can make their own decisions. Address any common errors.

- Give each learner photocopiable page 19 and ask them to circle the correct word in each sentence. Explain that there are many irregular plurals where the original word changes, for example mouse – mice; or both the singular and plural are the same, for example sheep – sheep. Allow the learners time to explore some of these words on the photocopiable page before rewriting the passage, changing single nouns into plurals. Remind them that it won't be just the nouns that change – pronouns and verbs may also be affected. For example:
  > The mouse was hiding in the bush. He was very afraid of the fox who lived in the wood.
  > The *mice were hiding* in the *bushes. They were* very afraid of the *foxes* who lived in the *woods.*

- Finally, ask them to read the passage out loud to check that it sounds right.

Top tips

Learners, particularly those with English as an additional language, are often confused by the various rules for pluralisation. Oral work, such as encouraging them to read passages aloud, can help to embed these rules and address the many irregularities that exist.

Study Guide

See pages 18–19 of the Study Guide for further revision of regular and irregular plurals and words ending in *o*.

Name: ______________________________

Plurals

Regular plurals

1 Circle the correct plural of the noun.

The **lions** / **liones** were sleeping in the **bushes** / **bushs**.

One of his **wishes** / **wishs** was to make a den out of **leafs** / **leaves**.

The **monkeys** / **monkies** were leaping around and frightening the **ladys** / **ladies**.

The horse's **hoofs** / **hooves** were clattering on the road.

Irregular plurals

2 Write the plurals of these nouns. Use a dictionary to help you if you are unsure.

tooth –	ox –	child –
sheep –	man –	foot –
mouse –	goose –	woman –
cactus –	deer –	fungus –

3 Rewrite this passage, making all the nouns plural. Take care to change other parts of the sentence where necessary. Read it aloud to check that it makes sense.

The mouse was hiding in the bush. He was very afraid of the fox who lived in the wood and the old lady who lived in the nearby house. A leaf trembled above his head, tickling his nose. Suddenly a deer appeared. The mouse had never seen this strange creature before. He was used to the sheep and the goose. The deer's hoof was very close to where the mouse was hiding. He kept very still. Maybe his wish would come true …

____

____

____

____

____

Quick quiz 1

1 The five vowels in the alphabet are _____. [5]

2 The long *a* sound can be made in six different ways. Write them in the table with an example word for each.

1 -ay	play	**4**	
2		**5**	
3		**6**	

[5]

3 *-tion* is a common letter string. Write down five words containing this string.

_____   _____   _____   _____   _____   [5]

4 Unstressed vowels are vowels that are written in words but are not said or are pronounced in an unusual way. Complete the words below with unstressed vowels. Take care when spelling these words.

a not the same – d_____ [1]

b necklaces, rings and bracelets – j_____ [1]

c not happy – m_____ [1]

d place where books are kept – l_____ [1]

5 Fill in the correct prefixes and suffixes:

Joe was feeling very _____happy. It had been raining all day and it had

been _____possible to go outside. _____fortunately he had been

sitting quiet_____ for hours, playing with his computer, and now he was

bored. He had been very care_____ not to make a fuss and when his

father _____turned home from work he was very grate_____ to Joe

for being so thought_____. He gave him the big_____ hug and

offered to take him to the match on Saturday as a special treat. [9]

Name: _____

6 Synonyms are _____. [1]

Antonyms are _____. [1]

Suggest three synonyms for each of these words:

a angry – _____ [1]

b hot – _____ [1]

c lovely – _____ [1]

Suggest three antonyms for each of these words:

d ugly – _____ [1]

e tired – _____ [1]

f happy – _____ [1]

7 Homophones are _____

_____ [1]

Write a sentence for each of these homophones:

sale / sail

a _____ [1]

b _____ [1]

due / dew

c _____ [1]

d _____ [1]

8 Write the plurals of these words:

library – _____   jelly – _____   mouse – _____

family – _____   leaf – _____   class – _____

deer – _____   goose – _____   person – _____   [9]

Quick quiz 1 answers

1 The five vowels in the alphabet are **a, e, i, o, u**.   [5]

2 The long *a* sound can be made in six different ways. Write them in the table
with an example word for each.

Examples include:

1 -ay	play	**4 ei**	rein
2 a–e	**gate**	**5 ea**	**great**
3 ai	**pain**	**6 eigh**	**weigh**

[5]

3 *-tion* is a common letter string. Write down five words containing this string.

Examples include:

station   **action**   **election**   **reaction**   **fraction**   **fiction**   [5]

4 Unstressed vowels are vowels that are written in words but are not said or
are pronounced in an unusual way. Complete the words below with unstressed
vowels. Take care when spelling these words.

    a not the same – d**ifferent**   [1]

    b necklaces, rings and bracelets – j**ewellery**   [1]

    c not happy – m**iserable**   [1]

    d place where books are kept – l**ibrary**   [1]

5 Fill in the correct prefixes and suffixes:

Joe was feeling very **un**happy. It had been raining all day and it had

been **im**possible to go outside. **Un**fortunately he had been

sitting quiet**ly** for hours, playing with his computer, and now he was

bored. He had been very care**ful** not to make a fuss and when his

father **re**turned home from work he was very grate**ful** to Joe

for being so thought**ful**. He gave him the big**gest** hug and

offered to take him to the match on Saturday as a special treat.   [9]

Revise for Cambridge Primary Checkpoint English Teacher's Guide © Hodder & Stoughton Ltd 2013

6 Synonyms are <u>**words with similar meanings**</u>. [1]

Antonyms are <u>**words with opposite meanings**</u>. [1]

Suggest three synonyms for each of these words:

Examples include:

a angry – <u>**cross, irritated, annoyed**</u> [1]

b hot – <u>**burning, boiling, sizzling**</u> [1]

c lovely – <u>**beautiful, attractive, gorgeous**</u> [1]

Suggest three antonyms for each of these words:

Examples include:

d ugly – <u>**pretty, beautiful, handsome**</u> [1]

e tired – <u>**lively, energetic, sparkling**</u> [1]

f happy – <u>**miserable, grumpy, sad**</u> [1]

7 Homophones are <u>**words that sound the same but are spelt differently**</u>. [1]

Write a sentence for each of these homophones:

sale / sail

Examples include:

a <u>**The man bought a new shirt in the sale.**</u> [1]

b <u>**I can't wait until we sail to France on the ferry.**</u> [1]

due / dew

Examples include:

c <u>**He was due to catch the plane at 4 o'clock.**</u> [1]

d <u>**The grass was sparkling in the morning dew.**</u> [1]

8 Write the plurals of these words:

library – <u>**libraries**</u>	jelly – <u>**jellies**</u>	mouse – <u>**mice**</u>
family – <u>**families**</u>	leaf – <u>**leaves**</u>	class – <u>**classes**</u>
deer – <u>**deer**</u>	goose – <u>**geese**</u>	person – <u>**people**</u> [9]

Grammar and punctuation

Nouns and pronouns

> **Learning objectives**
>
> - Spell and make correct use of possessive pronouns, e.g. *their, theirs, my, mine*. (5PSV3)
> - Use pronouns, making clear to what or to whom they refer. (5GPw6)
> - Revise different word classes. (6GPr2)

Let's revise!

- Revise the definition of a **noun**: a name of a person, a place or a thing.
- Remind the learners that nouns can be divided into groups:
  - **masculine noun** (refers to a male): boy, man, father
  - **feminine noun** (refers to a female): girl, woman, mother
  - **common noun** (refers to either a male or female): teacher, driver, doctor
  - **neuter noun** (refers to something that is neither male nor female): book, pen, rug
  - **proper noun** (refers to a specific person, place or thing): Tom, Paris, January
  - **collective noun** (refers to a group of something): crowd, team, flock.
- Revise the definition of a **noun phrase**: can be just a single noun or a group of words that function in the same way as a noun, for example: a lot of money.
- Point out that noun phrases can include a determiner, for example: *these* pencils, *that* child. Sometimes in noun phrases another noun is used to act like an adjective, for example: library book. Ask learners to think of some sentences that include examples of these two types of noun phrase.
- Revise the definition of **pronouns**: words that are used instead of the noun to avoid repetition, for example: it, he, she, they.
- Ask the learners to write down as many pronouns as they can in 30 seconds.
- Make a class list. Discuss when it is appropriate to use pronouns.
- Ask the learners to underline all the pronouns that demonstrate possession and encourage them to give examples of these being used in sentences, for example: 'his' – The boy went to look after his sheep.
- Ask the learners to complete photocopiable page 25 on the use of proper nouns and pronouns.

> **Top tips**
>
> - If learners have English as a second language, or a limited vocabulary, oral work on nouns and noun phrases is invaluable. Talking about pictures or artefacts will help to develop their vocabulary.
> - To help learners to remember vocabulary, play simple word games such as *Name those nouns*. Ask: 'How many nouns can you see in the room beginning with *s*?' In pairs, one learner says the words while the other keeps count. See who can get the most in one minute.

> **Study Guide**
>
> See pages 22–23 of the Study Guide for further work on nouns and noun phrases.

Name: _____

Nouns and pronouns

Read this story.

> Once upon a time, there was a girl. One day, she told her to visit her. She was walking along when she met him. He spoke to her but she walked on. He went ahead to visit her. She let him in. He locked her in the cupboard. When she arrived, he pretended to be her and tried to eat her, but luckily he rushed in and killed him.

1 Why is this story so difficult to understand?

_____

_____

_____

Now read this version of the story.

> Once upon a time, there was a girl named Little Red Riding Hood. One day, Little Red Riding Hood's mother told Little Red Riding Hood to visit Little Red Riding Hood's granny. Little Red Riding Hood was walking along when Little Red Riding Hood met the Big Bad Wolf. The Big Bad Wolf spoke to Little Red Riding Hood but Little Red Riding Hood walked on. The Big Bad Wolf went ahead of Little Red Riding Hood to visit Little Red Riding Hood's granny. Little Red Riding Hood's granny let the Big Bad Wolf in and the Big Bad Wolf locked Little Red Riding Hood's granny in the cupboard. When Little Red Riding Hood arrived, the Big Bad Wolf pretended to be Little Red Riding Hood's granny and tried to eat Little Red Riding Hood, but luckily the Woodcutter rushed in and killed the Big Bad Wolf.

2 What is wrong with this version?

_____

_____

_____

3 Rewrite the story, with the right balance of proper nouns and pronouns. Use nouns so that the reader knows who is doing what, but don't use them so many times in a row that it sounds repetitive. Read your version aloud to see if it makes sense.

Grammar and punctuation

Verbs

Learning objectives

- Confirm all parts of the verb *to be* and know when to use each one. (4PSV2)
- Investigate past, present and future tenses of verbs. (4GPr6)
- Experiment with varying tenses within texts, e.g. in dialogue. (4GPw3)
- Understand conventions of standard English, e.g. the agreement of verbs. (5GPr3)
- Explore uses of active and passive verbs. (6GPr6)

Let's revise!

- Revise the definition of a **verb:** a word that expresses an action – a 'doing', 'having' or 'being' word, for example: she *ran*, he *has*, I *am*.
- Ensure the learners are secure with using forms of the verb 'to be' – I am, we are, you are, he is, they are, I was, they were, and so on. If this knowledge is not secure, it should be developed through conversation, giving learners the opportunity to use the verb in its various forms.
- Remind the learners that the **tense** of the verb tells us *when* something is done. If necessary, discuss the definition of past, present and future and ask them to think of oral examples of each, for example: I walked to the shop yesterday – I am walking to the shop now – I will walk to the shop tomorrow.
- Revise that there are regular verbs that follow a pattern when changing tenses, for example: adding -*s*, -*ed* and -*ing*; and irregular verbs that we just have to learn, for example: say – said; go – went. You may also need to remind learners of how verbs change depending on who is doing it – first, second and third person, singular and plural, for example: I run, you run, she runs, they run.
- Discuss how, sometimes, two or more words make up a verb phrase, for example: are going, didn't want, has been waiting. Ask the learners to complete the table at the top of photocopiable page 27.
- Revise the definition of active and passive verbs:
    - **active:** the subject performs the action, for example: The boy chased the cat.
    - **passive:** the subject has the action done to it, for example: The cat was chased by the boy.
- Ask the learners to make and play *The loop game* on photocopiable page 27. This game could be adapted for wide range of content across the curriculum and is particularly useful for revision. For example, for science revision, put the question at the bottom of one card and the answer at the top of the next.

Top tips

- Most learners need to be reminded of the importance of making their verbs 'agree' (ensuring that the verb matches the subject) and of maintaining the consistency of the tense.
- Encourage the learners to read their work aloud to see if it sounds right.

Study Guide

See pages 24–25 of the Study Guide for investigations into tenses, active and passive forms and the use of imperative verbs.

Verbs

Complete this table.

Verb	Present tense	Past tense	Future tense
talk	I talk	I talked	I will talk
fly	I fly		
go			
sit			
write			
sleep			

The loop game

1 Divide a piece of A4 card into equal sections. It's up to you how many cards you decide to make: 9 (3 rows of 3), 12 (3 rows of 4), 16 (4 rows of 4), and so on.

2 At the *bottom* of the first box write a sentence with an active verb in it.

3 At the *top* of the next box write the same sentence but in the passive form.

The mountain was climbed by the man. The bird sang a lovely song.	A lovely song was sung by the bird. The girl ate the cake.	

4 At the *bottom* of that box write a new sentence with an active verb in it, and at the *top* of the next box write the same sentence in the passive form.

5 Fill all the boxes in the same way. When you get to the last box, write an active sentence at the bottom and then write its passive partner in at the top of the first box, creating a complete loop.

6 Cut up the cards, shuffle them and hand them round.

7 Anyone can start by reading the sentence at the bottom of their card.

8 The person who has the passive version must read it out, and then, straight away, read the sentence at the bottom of their card.

9 Keep going until you get back to the beginning. The person who started should be the person who finishes!

10 Time how long it takes to get back to the beginning and then try to beat your record.

Grammar and punctuation

Adverbs and adjectives

Let's revise!

- Revise the definition of **adverbs:** *add* to the verb, answering questions such as 'how', 'when' and 'where'; adverbs often end in *-ly*.
- Compile a classroom list of adverbs.
- Play *In the manner of the word*. Ask one learner to be the guesser who leaves the room and thinks of three everyday tasks. While the guesser is out of the room, the rest of the class decides on an adverb, for example: lazily, excitedly, grumpily, cautiously, carelessly. When the guesser re-enters the room he / she must ask someone in the class to perform one of the everyday tasks in the manner of the word. Repeat this with another learner and a different task, and then a third. Finally the guesser must guess the adverb.
- Revise the definition of an **adverbial phrase:** a group of words that functions in the same way as a single adverb, for example: a few days ago, on a regular basis, in a strange way.
- Revise the definition of an **adjective:** a word that describes somebody or something, for example: nervous, gloomy, miserable.
- Revise the definition of an **adjectival phrase:** a group of words that acts as extended descriptions of the noun, for example: black and white cat.
- Display some artefacts, for example: an ornament, an old toy, some unusual fruit; or show some pictures of artefacts and ask the learners to describe them using adjectives. Alternatively, make the artefact a mystery and find out if the learners can guess what the object is from your description, then encourage them to have a go with a different mystery artefact.
- Ask the learners to complete the task on adding descriptive language on photocopiable page 29.

Top tips

Encourage the learners to use a thesaurus regularly in order to expand their vocabulary and make choices about the best possible word for the piece of writing.

Study Guide

See pages 26–27 of the Study Guide for further work on comparative and superlative forms of adjectives.

Name: _____

Adverbs and adjectives

Adverbs and adjectives add detail and description to a piece of writing.

Turn these ordinary sentences into a scary story by adding some interesting descriptive vocabulary. You can even choose better verbs if you think it will improve the sentences, for example:

> The moon was shining in the sky.
> The ghostly moon was shimmering mysteriously in the midnight sky.

(There are so many wonderful words, try not to use the same one twice!)

The trees waved in the darkness.

_____

_____

_____

A sound could be heard in the distance.

_____

_____

_____

The wind blew through the window.

_____

_____

_____

A figure appeared in the shadows.

_____

_____

_____

A voice called my name.

_____

_____

_____

Grammar and punctuation

Prepositions

Learning objectives

- Identify prepositions and use the term. (5GPr2)
- Revise different word classes. (6GPr2)

Let's revise!

- Revise prepositions or prepositional phrases – words that indicate position:
  - **prepositions:** above, below, near, under, behind, on, past, through, to
  - **prepositional phrases** (two or more words that go together): next to, not far from, by the side of, close to, on top of.
- Give the learners one minute to write down as many prepositions or prepositional phrases as they can.
- Play *Preposition I-spy*. In pairs, one learner should choose a visible object in the room and then give up to five preposition clues, for example: it is near something blue. Each clue must contain a different preposition and the clue shouldn't give too much away at the beginning, for example: 'on top of the bookcase' might really narrow it down! After each clue, the partner is allowed one guess. Play the game a few times so that both learners have a go at describing where the object is in the room.
- Talk about the fact that some prepositions are more abstract, describing relative positions. This is a bit more challenging and harder to remember. For example:

  > These flowers are different *from* the ones in my garden but they are similar *to* the ones in your garden. However they are much better *than* the flowers next door.
  >
  > In fact, I prefer your garden *to* mine but, compared *with* next door, my garden still looks quite good!

- Ask the learners to complete the revision exercise on photocopiable page 31.

Top tips

- Learners are often unsure about which preposition to use with 'different' – 'from' or 'to'. They will often see the wrong preposition used in books, the press, adverts, conversation, and so on. The correct use is 'different from'.

- To ensure prepositional phrases become embedded, use speaking and listening games to draw the learners' attention to them and encourage oral rehearsal. To play *Pass it on*, for example, one learner starts by addressing another person: 'Katie, my shoes are different *from* your shoes'. Katie then says: 'That's true but, Stephen, my nose is different *from* your nose'. And so on, around the class.

Study Guide

See pages 28–29 of the Study Guide for further preposition exercises, including prepositions that might be added to a verb to change its meaning.

Name: _____

Prepositions

1 Write sentences that use the following prepositions.

  a behind

_____

  b through

_____

  c past

_____

  d near

_____

  e beside

_____

2 Write sentences that use the following prepositional phrases.

  a not far from

_____

_____

_____

  b in the same area as

_____

_____

_____

3 Complete this mini story using as many prepositions and prepositional phrases as possible. Try to keep it under 100 words and make sure that it makes sense! 📄

Under the bridge, right next to the stream, lived a troll. One day, he went …

Grammar and punctuation

Simple and compound sentences

Learning objectives

- Use a wider variety of connectives in an increasing range of sentences. (4GPw4)
- Explore ways of combining simple sentences and re-ordering clauses to make compound and complex sentences. (5GPw5)
- Investigate clauses within sentences and how they are connected. (5GPr5)
- Begin to show awareness of the impact of writers' choices of sentence length and structure. (6GPr4)

Let's revise!

- Remind the learners that sentence variation is very important when writing. It is vital to include short snappy sentences alongside longer, more complicated ones. Sentences can be simple, compound or complex (see page 34 for activities that revise complex sentences). Revise the following definitions:
  - **clause:** a group of words that expresses an event and usually contains a subject and a verb, for example: He followed the path (subject: He; verb: followed)
  - **simple sentence:** consists of one clause, for example: He got lost.
  - **compound sentence:** has two or more main clauses of equal weight, joined by one of these simple connectives (also called conjunctions): and, or, but, so; for example: He followed the path but he got lost.

- Play *Over to you* to revise the use of connectives and compound sentences. Begin by saying a simple sentence. The learners have to offer a connective – and, or, but, so – and a second clause to finish the sentence. For example:

  The teacher was old … but she could still do a cartwheel!
  The bus was late …
  The door was locked …
  The sandwich was mouldy …
  The cat was ugly …
  The baby was crying …

- Ask the learners to complete the revision activities on photocopiable page 33.

- Ask the learners to investigate whether the choice of connective can subtly alter the meaning of the sentence. For example, compare:

  The door was locked so he left.
  The door was locked and he left.

  The first sentence indicates that he had to leave because the door was locked, whereas the second one hints that because the door was locked, it was all right for him to leave.

  Ask the learners to find more examples of connectives altering the meaning of sentences.

Top tips

In order that the learners understand the difference between compound and complex sentences, it is important that they realise that the clauses in compound sentences need to be of equal weight and can stand alone as separate sentences. For example: He wanted to keep fit – (so) – He walked to school.

Study Guide

See pages 30–31 of the Study Guide for further exercises on simple and compound sentences.

Name: _____

Compound sentences

1 Match the clauses to make compound sentences.

The tiger prowled all night	but he didn't like pasta.
Mrs Smith taught us English	so he was locked in the cage.
I might go to the library	and it looked very threatening.
Grandpa was cold	but he was late.
The sky was black	and Mr Jones taught us Maths.
John was going swimming	or I might read at home.
My teacher was hungry	so I gave him a coat.

2 The order in which the two clauses are written, and the choice of connective, can slightly alter the meaning.

Join combinations of two of these simple sentences in different ways to explore different meanings.

> She heard a noise. She stopped. She looked around. She kept walking. Her heart was pounding. She was alone. She wasn't worried. She felt faint. She sat down.

For example:

She looked around but she was alone.
She was alone so she looked around.

_____

_____

_____

_____

_____

_____

Grammar and punctuation

Complex sentences

Learning objectives

- Use a wider variety of connectives in an increasing range of sentences. (4GPw4)
- Use an increasing range of subordinating connectives and investigate their meaning and spelling. (5GPw4, 6PSV7)
- Investigate the use of conditionals, e.g. to express possibility. (6GPr3)
- Distinguish the main clause and other clauses in a complex sentence. (6GPr8)
- Use a wider range of connectives to clarify relationships between ideas, e.g. *however, therefore*, although. (6GPw2)
- Develop grammatical control of complex sentences, manipulating them for effect. (6GPw4)
- Develop increasing accuracy in using punctuation effectively to mark out the meaning in complex sentences. (6GPw5)

Let's revise!

- Revise what is meant by a **complex sentence:** has a **main clause** and a *subordinate clause* to add extra detail. The clauses are often joined by a <u>connective</u> other than *and, but, or, so*. The subordinate clause is often embedded (dropped in) and held in place by two commas. For example:

  The lion, *who had been sleeping peacefully in the long grass*, **began to stir**.
  <u>Although</u> *the snow was falling quite heavily*, **the explorer continued across the ice**.

- Play the *Complex sentence game*:
  - Arrange the class into mixed-ability groups.
  - Make a set of instruction cards (see right) for each group, cut them up and place a set on each table, face down.
  - Write a complex sentence on the board, for example: As I leant against the fence, it broke. ('It [the fence] broke' – main clause; I leant against it – subordinate clause.) A learner in the first group should pick a card and read the instruction. The first group decides what they will do to the sentence on the board.
  - The other groups also decide what they would do, in case there is an opportunity to steal the points if the first group gets it wrong.
  - Award appropriate points – the first group to ten points wins.

- Explain that complex sentences can also be created using a 'conditional subordinate clause' to show possibility. For example: If you shut the gate, the horses won't escape. 'If you shut the gate' states the condition, contains a verb but does not make sense on its own.

- Discuss the range of connectives that might be used in a complex sentence and ask the learners to complete photocopiable page 35 for further practice on using these in complex sentences.

Create a completely new complex sentence. 6 points	Change the subject in the main clause. 6 points
Move the subordinate clause. 6 points	Change the first word (or phrase) of the subordinate clause. 4 points
Change the subordinate clause. 4 points	Change the main clause. 2 points
Change the verb in the main clause. 2 points.	Miss a turn. 0 points

Top tips

Show the learners that a number of short, simple sentences, used alongside more elaborate sentences, can create tension, for example: He stopped. He waited. It was getting closer. He turned around and there, standing before him, was the slimy green monster with the saucer-like eyes. He couldn't move.

Study Guide

See pages 32–33 of the Study Guide for further practice on complex sentences.

Name: _____

Complex sentences

1 Make a list of connectives you might use when writing complex sentences. Some may be phrases. The list has been started for you.

after   because   while
although   as long as

2 Choose five of your connectives and include them in complex sentences.

Try to vary the order of the words in the sentences, for example the connective may come at the beginning or in the middle.

Make sure you include commas.

a _____

_____

_____

_____

b _____

_____

_____

_____

c _____

_____

_____

_____

d _____

_____

_____

_____

e _____

_____

_____

_____

Grammar and punctuation

Commas

Let's revise!

• Remind the learners of the purpose of **punctuation**: helps the reader to make sense of the writing, and read it in the way the writer intended.

• Revise the use of commas to divide different parts of a sentence and make the meaning of the sentence clearer. Write the following sentence on the board and ask the learners to read it to themselves with the comma and then read it without. Ask them to explain what the comma is doing.

> As part of our food project, we had to do lots of tasting.
> (comma used after subordinate clause)

Do the same with these three sentences:

> Our teacher brought in a mango, a papaya, a kiwi fruit and a fresh coconut for us to try.
> (commas used to separate items in a list)

> However, I had already tasted them all before.
> (comma used following a connective)

> Meg, the one with the nut allergy, decided not to risk it.
> (comma used as a parenthesis – to add extra information)

• Write this sentence on the board without the punctuation and ask the learners to write it down, putting the commas where they think they should go.

> The bird, which had blue, green and red feathers, sang a lovely song, even though it was trapped in a cage.

Discuss the comma after the word 'song'. Explain that the comma is there to separate the clauses and allow time for a pause.

• Ask the learners to complete the revision activity on photocopiable page 37.

Name: _____

Commas

Read this passage out loud. You must read it exactly as it is punctuated!

Mr Monroe who had travelled from America was extremely tired. Arriving at the hotel he was much too late for dinner so he ordered some coffee fruit rolls and water to be delivered to his room. The room which overlooked the river was much too warm but the window refused to open. However when the waiter brought the food up to the room he was able to turn the heating down for Mr Monroe. Unfortunately within an hour Mr Monroe was much too cold. As he couldn't work out the heating system himself he just decided to put on his hat coat scarf and gloves and sit under his quilt. Luckily he soon fell asleep.

Did you realise that 'America was extremely tired' or that you could order such a thing as 'coffee fruit rolls'?

Rewrite the passage above, punctuating it correctly.

_____

_____

_____

_____

_____

_____

_____

_____

_____

_____

_____

_____

_____

Now, read the passage aloud and check that the commas are doing what you want them to do.

Grammar and punctuation

Apostrophes

Learning objectives

- Learn the use of the apostrophe to show possession and shortened forms. (4GPr3, 5GPw2)
- Punctuate speech and use apostrophes accurately. (6GPw1)

Let's revise!

- To orally rehearse the use of possessive apostrophes and contractions, play the game *Passing the blame*:
  - Begin by saying, with expression: This is the worst piece of work I've ever marked – it must be John's work. (Pick a name from the class.)
  - John then says: That's not my scruffy work – it must be Ahmed's work.
  - Ahmed then says: That's not my untidy work – it must be Amandeep's work.
  - Amandeep then says: That's definitely not my disgusting work – it must be Shivi's work.
  - Shivi then says: I can assure you that's not my scruffy work – it must be … and so on.
- The learners can embellish the sentence as they wish but the basic structure must stay the same.
- Vary the opening sentence to make the game fun, for example:

  This is the silliest hat *I've* ever seen – it must be *Maryam's* hat.

  This is the untidiest bedroom *I've* ever been in – it must be *Rui's* room.

  That was the worst meal *I've* ever eaten – it must be *Lola's* cooking.

- When everyone has had a turn, write your opening sentence on the board:

  This is the worst piece of work *I've* ever marked – it must be *John's* work.

- Ask the learners to discuss with a partner the two uses of the apostrophe:

  I've – a **contraction** – short for 'I have' – denotes missing letters

  John's – **possessive** – the work belongs to John.

- Choose someone to explain the rules to the class.
- Write some more examples of sentences using apostrophes correctly and incorrectly. Encourage the learners to identify the different uses and explain why they are correct or incorrect.
- Ask the learners to complete the activities on photocopiable page 39.

Top tips

- Incorrect use of the apostrophe is very common. It is often used incorrectly with the addition of an 's' to denote the plural. For example, *animal's crossing* should be *animals crossing* (unless the crossing belongs to an animal), *lots of bird's* should be *lots of birds*. Encourage the learners, before using an apostrophe, to ask the question 'Does anything belong to this noun?' If the answer is no, an apostrophe is not needed.
- Provide opportunities for learners to identify when apostrophes are needed. For example, say a phrase or sentence and ask the learners to repeat it. If there is an apostrophe they should draw an imaginary apostrophe in the air as they say the word where the apostrophe appears.
- Point out that contractions should only be used in informal writing or when writing speech.

Study Guide

See pages 36–37 of the Study Guide for further examples of correct use of apostrophes and extension work on variation in the position of the possessive apostrophe.

Name: _____

Apostrophes

1 These sentences don't look quite right. Try writing them out again below.

Ive always wanted to have a go on Matthews bike but hes so possessive he wont let anyone ride it. Its not fair.

_____

_____

_____

2 Have a go at turning these around. For example:

The hat that belongs to Mum – Mum's hat.

a The sweets that belong to Nora – _____

b The house where Mr Sharma lives – _____

c The scary look a teacher gives you – _____

3 How many contractions can you think of? Write them in the box below with the full version. Underline those where the word changes.

I've – I have

it's – it is

<u>won't</u> – <u>will not</u>

Grammar and punctuation

Direct and reported speech

Let's revise!

- To revise the difference between direct and reported speech, play the *He said, she said* game. Ask the learners to get into groups of three and label themselves A, B and C. A and C have had an argument and they are not speaking to each other. B is the go-between:
  - A tells B something, for example: I'm not speaking to him because he crashed my new bike.
  - B then has to relay the sentence, for example: He said that he's not speaking to you because you crashed his new bike.
  - C then replies, for example: It wasn't me who crashed it!
  - B says, for example: He said that it wasn't him who crashed it! And so on …
- Discuss the difference between direct speech and reported speech. A and C are both using direct speech, whereas B in the middle is using reported speech (reporting what has been said, after the event).
- Model how a conversation could be written down in two ways. For example:
  - 'It wasn't me who crashed your bike,' explained Mel. (direct speech)
  - Mel explained that it wasn't him who had crashed the bike. (reported speech)

  Revise the correct placement of the speech marks and the comma in the first sentence.
- Before looking at photocopiable page 41, ask the learners to write down some rules they could give to younger writers on how to punctuate direct speech and then some rules for reported speech. Discuss these.
- Compare these rules with the ones on photocopiable page 41 and ask the learners to complete the exercise.

Top tips

- Create a display of words and phrases that could be used in direct speech. For example, bellowed, moaned, whispered nervously, boomed like a cannon, croaked in a frog-like voice. Encourage the learners to add to this whenever they come across a good word or phrase whilst reading.
- Encourage the learners to write phrases used in direct speech in an author's notebook as a method of recording ideas for later use in written work.

Study Guide

See pages 38–39 of the Study Guide for more practice in punctuating direct and reported speech.

Name: _____

Direct and reported speech

Some rules for speech

Direct speech	Reported speech
Start a new line for each new speaker.	You don't have to start a new line for each speech.
Start what is being said with a capital letter.	It is written in the past tense as it is reporting what has been said. For example: He comment*ed* on the fact that it's cold in here.
If the sentence is interrupted, the next part begins with a small letter. For example: 'But,' moaned Shivi, 'it doesn't make sense.'	You can change the verb used to describe how something was said. For example: 'I'm not going!' <u>muttered</u> Lou. Lou <u>told</u> them that he was not going.
The end punctuation goes inside the speech marks.	First person changes to third person. For example: 'I think it's cold in here.' He said he thinks it's cold in here.

1 Change this conversation from direct speech to reported speech.

> 'Where is your homework?' boomed Mr Lang.
>
> 'An enormous bear attacked me on the way to school and ran off with it in its paw,' stammered Ravi.
>
> Mr Lang laughed. 'You expect me to believe that?' he asked, sarcastically.

2 Now change the following paragraph from reported speech to direct speech.

> Just then Mr Nadal, the caretaker, walked in and said that he had just seen a huge bear running around the school field. Mr Lang was quite surprised and asked if the bear was carrying anything in its paw. Mr Nadal told them that he had seen something white in its paw. He said it had looked like some sheets of paper. Ravi smiled.

Grammar and punctuation

Using a range of punctuation

Learning objectives

- Use knowledge of punctuation and grammar to read with fluency, understanding and expression and respond to punctuation marks when reading. (4GPr1, 4GPr2)

- Use a range of end-of-sentence punctuation with accuracy, re-reading own writing to check punctuation and grammatical sense. (4GPw1, 4GPw5)

- Identify uses of the colon, semi-colon, parenthetic commas, dashes and brackets. (6GPr1)

Let's revise!

- Ask the learners to write down as many different punctuation symbols as they can think of and discuss when they might be used.
- Revise the subtle difference between using parenthetic commas, brackets and dashes:
  - **commas:** when adding extra information that is fairly essential to the sentence:

    The boy, who had just moved to Britain from Australia, was finding it hard to fit in.

  - **brackets:** when adding information that is less essential, and could even be missed out. The brackets separate the information from the rest of the sentence:

    The youngest child (the one who often wears a hat) was sitting in the back of the car.

  - **dashes:** when adding information in informal writing:

    My brother – who can't sing for toffee – has just joined the choir!

  Ask the learners to think of a sentence that demonstrates one of the above. Choose a few learners to say their sentence. Ask others to decide whether it uses commas, brackets or dashes.

- Revise the use of colons and semi-colons:
  - **semi-colon:** stronger than a comma, but not as strong as a full stop and may be used instead of a connective to separate parts of a sentence:

    David likes to ski; Sam prefers to snowboard.

  - **colon:** sometimes used before someone speaks or to introduce a list or a set of bullet points:

    Dan said: 'I'm not coming to the park.'
    You will need: a warm coat, sturdy shoes and a torch.

  Ask the learners to write down one sentence in the style of each of the examples, making sure that colons and semi-colons are used correctly.

- Discuss the use of end-of-sentence punctuation marks:
  - **?** (when asking a question)
  - **!** (to show strong feeling, for example surprise, anger, joy; or shouting)
  - **...** (ellipses – in place of missing words, to indicate a pause or a mystery / cliffhanger)

  Ask the learners to write down a sentence for each one.

- Ask the learners to complete the revision exercises on photocopiable page 43.

Top tips

Encourage the learners always to read their work through, preferably aloud, and double check punctuation marks. They should then ask someone else to read it aloud, and if it isn't read as it was intended, they should review the punctuation.

Study Guide

See pages 40–41 of the Study Guide for further exercises on the full range of punctuation.

Using a range of punctuation

Punctuation helps to make the meaning clear, so it is useful to have a range at your fingertips.

Parenthetic commas, brackets and dashes

> , parenthetic commas,
>
> **(**brackets**)**
>
> – dashes –

1   Choose the most appropriate method of punctuating the additional information and add it in to these sentences.

   a   Mia whose pet had been missing for two days was unable to stop crying all day.

   b   The male lion with the enormous mane was pacing up and down.

   c   At the weekend and it can't come too soon we are going to the beach.

   d   My Maths teacher the one who lives near Julie said I should get full marks.

   e   After school thank goodness my mum is taking me to get my hair cut.

Colons and semi-colons

2   Fill in the missing colons (**:**) and semi-colons (**;**).

   a   It was very icy the pavement was slippery.

   b   The actor boomed 'The coast is clear. We must be quick.'

   c   A new puppy will need a cosy bed two bowls a small collar and lead special puppy food and a lot of attention.

   d   Sofia has a sweet tooth Sara prefers savoury things.

Question marks, exclamation marks or ellipses

3   Punctuate this passage correctly.

   Oh no Which way should he go As he peered into the darkness he saw

Name: _____   Total: _____ / 33

Quick quiz 2

1 Underline the noun phrases in these sentences:

   a I forgot to pick up those soup spoons from Gran.   [1]

   b I can't believe that Mr Jones gave us a load of homework for the weekend.   [1]

2 Change these verbs from active to passive:

   a The cow jumped over the moon.

   _____ [1]

   b The younger team beat the older team in the final race.

   _____ [1]

3 Change the adjectives, the verb and the adverb to make three different sentences.
The <u>scruffy</u> boy <u>scurried excitedly</u> down the <u>steep</u> path.

   a _____ [1]

   b _____ [1]

   c _____ [1]

4 Write five prepositions.

   a _____   **b** _____   **c** _____

   d _____   **e** _____   [5]

   Now write a sentence for each one.

   f _____ [1]

   g _____ [1]

   h _____ [1]

   i _____ [1]

   j _____ [1]

Name: _____

5 Improve this passage. You must get all the information into a maximum of
four good sentences. Try not to use 'and' more than twice! [4]

> Bob was a mouse. He lived in a tiny hole. Bob loved cheese. He would
> sneak out every evening. He would search for cheese. Sometimes he
> would be lucky. He would pounce on it. He would eat it as quickly as
> he could. Sometimes he would not be lucky. He would go back to his
> hole. He would feel quite sad.

_____

_____

_____

_____

_____

6 Put the commas into these sentences.

  a I want to buy a new pen some new pencils and some coloured crayons for school.

  b Jack who was only ten years old had just taken the running record for the
  fastest time.

  c Unfortunately the house we wanted to buy was sold.

  d If you want to get good marks you have to put in the practice. [4]

7 Put apostrophes into these sentences.

  a Have you been peeking at Dans presents?

  b Ive got so much to do I dont think Ill be able to come to the party [2]

8 Rewrite this passage, changing the reported speech into direct speech. 📄

> Pam looked up and saw Mim walk into the cafe. Mim asked if she could
> come and sit by her while she waited for her mother to arrive. Pam
> answered, rather apologetically, that she was sorry but she was waiting
> for her friends to join her. Mim looked disappointed and started to walk
> away. Pam felt guilty so she called out to her that it was OK and she could
> sit there for a few minutes. Mim smiled, said thank you and sat down. [6]

Quick quiz 2 answers

1 Underline the noun phrases in these sentences.

   a I forgot to pick up **those soup spoons** from Gran. [1]

   b I can't believe that Mr Jones gave us **a load of homework** for the weekend. [1]

2 Change these verbs from active to passive.

   a The cow jumped over the moon. [1]

   The moon was jumped over by the cow.

   b The younger team beat the older team in the final race. [1]

   In the final race, the older team was beaten by the younger team.

3 Change the adjectives, the verb and the adverb to make three different sentences.

The scruffy boy scurried excitedly down the steep path.

Examples include:

   a The **agile** boy **raced enthusiastically** down the **narrow** path. [1]

   b The **lazy** boy **sauntered slowly** down the **weedy** path. [1]

   c The **exhausted** boy **stepped gingerly** down the **treacherous** path. [1]

4 Write five prepositions.

   a–e Examples include: in, on, under, over, past, near, before, after, behind, beside, among, to [5]

Now write a sentence for each one.

Examples include:

   f The crocodile lay just under the surface of the water. [1]

   g The house was built near the road. [1]

   h The plate was put on the table. [1]

   i The girl sat down beside her sister. [1]

   j The car drove over the bridge. [1]

 Revise for Cambridge Primary Checkpoint English Teacher's Guide © Hodder & Stoughton Ltd 2013

5 Improve the passage. You must get all the information into a maximum of four good sentences. Try not to use 'and' more than twice! [4]

For example:

Bob, a mouse who lived in a tiny hole, loved cheese. Every evening, he would sneak out in search of cheese. Sometimes he would be lucky, pouncing on it and eating it as quickly as he could. Sometimes, however, he would not be so lucky and he would go sadly back to his hole.

6 Put the commas into these sentences.

a I want to buy a new pen, some new pencils and some coloured crayons for school.

b Jack, who was only ten years old, had just taken the running record for the fastest time.

c Unfortunately, the house we wanted to buy was sold.

d If you want to get good marks, you have to put in the practice. [4]

7 Put apostrophes into these sentences.

a Have you been peeking at Dan's presents?

b I've got so much to do I don't think I'll be able to come to the party. [2]

8 Rewrite the passage, changing the reported speech into direct speech.

For example:
Pam looked up and saw Mim walk into the cafe.
'Can I sit here while I wait for my mother to arrive?' Mim asked.
'Sorry,' Pam answered, rather apologetically, 'but I'm waiting for my friends to join me.'
Mim looked disappointed and started to walk away. Pam felt guilty.
'It's OK!' she called out. 'You can sit here for a few minutes.'
'Thanks,' said Mim gratefully. She sat down. [6]

Reading

Historical stories – settings

Let's revise!

- For the following activities, use the example narrative on photocopiable page 49.
- Read up to 'They were ...' on photocopiable page 49 together. It is the beginning of a short story called *Fire!* by Stephanie Austwick. It is set in London, in 1666, during the Great Fire of London.
- Revise the definition of a **genre:** a category or type of literature, for example: adventure, historical, science fiction.
- Ask the learners to decide on the genre of the text (historical) and discuss the clues sprinkled through the text that tell us that it is set in the past. For example:
  - the names: Mary, Old Samuel
  - the setting: straw mattress; narrow, cobbled street; thatched roof; candlelight
  - the language: casement.
- Revise the definition of a setting. Using the text on photocopiable page 49, explore as a class how the author has created the setting, with a focus on language features:
  - proper nouns: London
  - adjectives: *old, straw* mattress; *narrow, cobbled* street – discuss the use of commas in a list
  - alliteration: *Recently, the rancid air had wrapped around*
  - personification: a candle flickering nervously; light creeping stealthily
  - similes: like a thick cloak.
- Ask the learners to comment on how this language helps to 'paint' the scene. Invite suggestions of when or where this might be taking place (London, 1666).

- Look again at the text on photocopiable page 49 and discuss the reference to different senses, for example: scratchy straw, flickering candle, faint crackling, hint of smoke. Ask the learners to discuss what effect this has on the reader. For example, by appealing to the different senses, it helps the scene to come to life for the reader; the reader makes connections with their own experiences.
- Ask the learners to read the remainder of the text on photocopiable page 49 and answer the questions independently.
- For further revision of the importance of picking up on the historical clues in this genre, invite the learners to act out an interview with Mary as she describes the scene on the night of the fire. Encourage them to use the first person, take facts from the text and choose language that makes the scene come to life for the audience, for example: strong adjectives, a variety of verbs and adverbs, similes – 'Nervously, I gripped the casement. The flames were leaping like ..., I heard ..., I saw...'
- This activity could be done with any historical text, and is particularly effective when linked to a period of history being covered in other areas of the curriculum.

Top tips

Demonstrate how to mark a text when reading, for example highlighting key words or key information on setting or characters, or genre clues. This is a useful revision tool.

Study Guide

Pages 44–45 of the Study Guide contain another extract from a historical story, encouraging further exploration of setting descriptions.

Name: _____

Historical stories – settings

Fire!

Mary stirred. The old, straw mattress scratched her bare arms. Silently, she crept towards the open casement, desperate for some air.

As she looked out across the thatched London skyline, she felt uneasy.

She could see a candle flickering nervously in the room opposite. Old Samuel never slept. Even Mary had found it difficult on these warm nights. Recently, the rancid air had wrapped around the timber buildings like a thick cloak, clinging to every surface. It had been suffocating.

But tonight felt different. Tonight there was breeze.

Mary leant a little further forward to study the narrow, cobbled street below.

Another light caught her eye. An orange glow, creeping stealthily between the houses.

Then a noise – a faint crackling – and just a hint of smoke in the air.

Mary held her breath and listened.

A shout rang out, echoing through the sleeping street. The word everyone dreaded – **'FIRE!'**

They were used to fires. The wardens were constantly patrolling the streets with leather buckets full of river water. The combination of wooden houses, warm weather, dry straw and candles was not a good one, but usually the fires were doused before they could get a hold.

Tonight was different! Tonight there was a breeze. The welcome breeze that everyone had longed for was now fanning the flames in the rooms below. They were already licking the side of the building, like the many tongues of some gigantic monster.

Mary knew she had to act quickly. It was too late to escape downstairs.

She began to climb through the open casement. At full stretch, she could just reach the room opposite.

Suddenly Old Samuel was there, grabbing her hand and helping her to safety.

'We must hurry, child,' he said. 'The flames will soon be here too. We will head for the river. It's our only hope.'

1 What 'combination' led to frequent fires? _____

_____

2 What effect did the breeze have? _____

3 How does the author describe the flames? _____

4 Write a short description of the setting for this story. 🗒

Reading

Fantasy stories – characters

Let's revise!

- Read the extract on photocopiable page 51 from *Rebecca's World* by Terry Nation – a fantasy narrative. Alternatively, use any suitable extract from a fantasy narrative and adapt the following activities accordingly. Ask the learners to point out clues that this is a fantasy story, for example ghostly creatures, superheroes.

- Ask the learners to discuss their first impressions of the character (Captain K). Then ask them, in pairs, to read the passage again and highlight or underline all the information about the character. Explore the difference between what they know and what can be inferred. For example:
  - his clothes seem three sizes too big – he looks rather weak and scrawny
  - he makes an 'achy groan' as he gets up – he has hurt himself, he's not good at 'flying'.

  Discuss the fact that we use prior knowledge and experience to help us make sense of these inferences.

- Ask the learners to underline or highlight any descriptive words or phrases in the text.

  Revise by discussing the effect of the language on the reader. For example:
  - adjectives: achy groans
  - adjectival phrases: three sizes too big for him
  - adverbs: slowly
  - adverbial phrases: with a rather grand gesture
  - similes: like a jelly falling from a great height; like a soap bubble.

- Ask the learners, in pairs, to build a character, using the details in the text and discussions around inferred information. To do this, they should draw a simple outline of a man. Around the outside they should write everything to do with the character's outward appearance, for example his clothes, his actions, his movements. On the inside, they should write everything that has been discussed about his character, feelings, personality, and so on.

Name: _____

Fantasy stories – characters

Rebecca stared up the high walls to the edge of the roof. Perched there was a figure of a man. He was dressed all in red. She had no time to catch more than a glimpse of him before he launched himself off the roof and dived headlong towards her, his little red cloak floating out behind him.

He hit the ground just in front of Rebecca with a sound like jelly falling from a great height. He gave a moan of pain and said, 'Splattt!' Then, with a few achy groans, he got to his feet, shook himself, and turned to face the GHOSTS.

From his belt, he pulled what looked like a stick. It was not much thicker than a finger and half as long as his arm. He waved it around like a sword.

The GHOSTS stopped in their tracks and made angry hissing noises. The man in red moved towards them, waving the stick and jabbing it at the GHOSTS. As he advanced, he shouted, 'Pow! … Zapp! … Zonk! … Kerchowww!'

To Rebecca's delight the GHOSTS started to back away. Slowly at first but then, as panic gripped them, faster and faster. The man jabbed his stick at the nearest GHOST. There was a loud, wet popping sound and it vanished like a soap bubble. The remaining GHOSTS turned and fled.

The scarlet figure followed them up to the corner and watched until all the GHOSTS had disappeared. Then he turned and started back to where Rebecca was standing.

She had the first chance to take a good look at him. He wore black boots and red tights. He had a long-sleeved T-shirt in the same colour red and, on his head, was what looked like a tight-fitting Balaclava helmet. Over his eyes was a red mask, and over that, a pair of spectacles.

He would have looked quite smart except that all the clothes seemed about three sizes too big for him. The tights and T-shirt were wrinkled and baggy. There were a few darns here and there, which had been made with wool that didn't exactly match. The bit of his face that Rebecca could see underneath the mask seemed quite nice and friendly.

He smiled at Rebecca.

'Once more the forces of evil have been vanquished,' he announced. His voice was a bit high and pipey.

from *Rebecca's World* by Terry Nation

Using all the information you have gathered about the man in red, write a full description of the character. Use interesting adjectives and adverbs to 'paint the picture'. 📓

Reading

Stories from other cultures – inference and atmosphere

Learning objectives

- Read widely and explore the features of different fiction genres. (4Rf1, 5Rf1)
- Understand how expressive and descriptive language creates mood. (4Rf9)
- Provide accurate textual reference from more than one point in a story to support answers to questions. (5Rf2)
- Discuss metaphorical expressions and figures of speech. (5Rf6)
- Look for implicit meanings, and make plausible inferences based on more than one point in the text. (6Rf3)
- Articulate personal responses to reading, with close reference to the text. (6Rf11)

Let's revise!

- Revise what is meant by 'from another culture'. Explore why it is important to learn about other cultures. Ask the learners to discuss any places they may have visited, or read about, or seen on television, which are different from their own environment.

- Give the learners time to look at a range of books covering different countries, religions, costumes, festivals, and so on. Remind them that culture is not just about the geography. Discuss the sorts of clues we should look out for if we are to tell if a story is from another culture and revise the definition of 'genre' if necessary.

- Read the extract on photocopiable page 53 either as a class or individually. Do not tell the learners that this is from *Journey to Johannesburg* by Beverley Naidoo. Ask the learners to look for clues in the text that hint at the setting and the characters. Explore some of the answers, pointing out that there are some things we are only guessing at this point. Discuss the term 'inference' – using clues and hints. Make it clear that it is appropriate for people to have different ideas and interpretations. Discuss how the learners think each character might be feeling at different points of the story. Ask them to discuss what they think might happen next and what makes them think that.

- Ask the learners to underline the clues then answer the questions, focusing on how the inference has added to the atmosphere created in this extract.

Top tips

The skills of inference and deduction can be developed in a fun way by using film clips and photographs, using the visual references as prompts. Encourage the learners to ask questions such as: 'What do you know?', 'What do you think you know?', 'What are the clues?', 'How has the atmosphere been created?' and 'What will happen next?' The same skills can then be transferred to written texts.

Study Guide

See pages 48–49 of the Study Guide for further work on description and atmosphere.

Stories from other cultures – using inference

On they walked. The sun was low down now and there was a smell of oranges coming from the rows and rows of orange trees behind barbed-wire fences. As far as they could see there were orange trees with dark green leaves and bright round fruit. Oranges were sweet and wonderful to taste and they didn't have them very often.

The children looked at each other.

'Do you think we could …' Tiro began.

But Naledi was already carefully pushing apart the barbed wire, edging her body through.

'Keep watch!' she ordered Tiro.

She was up on tiptoes, stretching for an orange, when they heard, HEY YOU!

Naledi dropped down, then dashed for the fence. Tiro was holding the wires for her. She tried to scramble through, but it was too late.

A hand grasped her and pulled her back.

Naledi looked up and saw a young boy, her own age.

'What are you doing?' he demanded.

He spoke in Tswana, their own language.

'The white farmer could kill you. Don't you know he has a gun to shoot thieves?'

1 Why is there a barbed-wire fence?

_____

2 Why do you think that the children do not have oranges very often?

_____

3 After the shout of 'HEY YOU!', how does the author create a feeling of panic?

_____

_____

_____

4 Will the boy be friendly or is something bad about to happen? Write your version of the next part of the story in the style of the extract.

Reading

Stories with issues – authors and viewpoints

Let's revise!

- Collect a number of books that deal with a variety of issues you may have studied in class. These issues should be appropriate to the learners, for example environmental issues, arguments between friends, poverty, animals in captivity. Discuss the sorts of issues raised in these books. Ask the learners why it is important to read and talk about these issues. **Be sensitive to the learners in the class and the culture of your school and country. Read the books first (before the learners) and if you think a particular book is not suitable, choose an alternative.**

- Discuss with the learners how works of fiction can sometimes allow readers to explore these issues more deeply and empathise with the situations.

- Read the extract on photocopiable page 55 with the class. It is taken from *Running Wild* by Michael Morpurgo and is set during the time of the Boxing Day Tsunami in 2004 – an area for discussion in its own right. The extract deals with the issue of hunting and the captivity of a tiger and young orang-utans. Ask the learners for their first impressions of this extract. Discuss how the author has managed to evoke strong feelings in his readers, for example by making the orang-utans 'little' and using harsh words like 'jabbing' and 'poking'.

- Re-read the extract and discuss viewpoint – the difference between author (Morpurgo) and narrator (the boy in the cage). In this case, the story is being written from the point of view of the narrator. Ask the learners to answer the questions on the passage on photocopiable page 55.

- Encourage the learners to read other books by Michael Morpurgo and discuss the issues raised in these books.

Top tips

● When revising emotive language used in stories that raise issues, encourage the learners to build up their own thesaurus exploring degrees of intensity, for example: push, nudge, prod, poke, jab – jab is stronger and therefore creates more emotion in the reader.

● Use whole-class circle time to encourage discussion of issues raised within these stories. The learners need to understand the importance of discussion – an opportunity to air personal feelings on emotive issues, while respecting the views of others.

Study Guide

See pages 50–51 of the Study Guide for a further example of a story with issues.

Name: _____

Stories with issues

The gathering crowd looked on in awe as the tiger passed by, but this soon turned to mocking laughter when they spotted me, and the little orang-utans, in the cage. They rattled the bars with sticks, poking and jabbing at us. They made monkey faces at us, and some of the children were laughing at us, sticking their tongues out. Everywhere there was whooping and yelling, and shooting too. They were firing their rifles off over our heads in celebration. With every shot the orang-utans clung tighter to me, pushing their faces into my chest, into my armpits, my neck, desperate for somewhere to hide.

from *Running Wild* by Michael Morpurgo

1 How does reading this extract make you feel and why?

_____

_____

2 Why do you think the tiger, the narrator and the baby orang-utans were in a cage?

_____

_____

3 Who is telling the story and how do you think the narrator is feeling?

_____

_____

4 How does the author create the atmosphere in this extract?

_____

_____

_____

5 How do you feel about the hunting of endangered animals?

_____

_____

_____

6 Imagine you were an onlooker, watching this scene. Describe what you saw. Try to make your viewpoint clear to the reader. 📑

Reading

Fables, myths and legends – the parts of a story

Learning objectives

- Understand the main stages of a story from introduction to resolution. (4Rf6)
- Explore narrative order and the focus on significant events. (4Rf7)
- Read and identify characteristics of myths, legends and fables. (5Rf9)
- Understand aspects of narrative structure. (6Rf4)

Let's revise!

- Revise the definitions of fables, myths and legends. They are all genres of stories with a history of oral tradition, which have been handed down from the past, although there are also modern versions. There are many definitions but the learners need to know that each type of story has special features:
  - **fable:** short story; untrue; often involves animals; teaches a moral at the end
  - **myth:** can be a longer story; often includes monsters, gods, heroes and villains, talking animals, and so on; untrue; can sometimes be used to explain a natural phenomenon
  - **legend:** can be a longer story; may not be true but is based on truth, such as a real person, place or event, but may have been added to and embellished over time.
- Read a range of examples to the class, for example: Aesop's fables, Creation myths, the legend of Robin Hood – or a similar local traditional story.
- Revise the fact that many stories can be split into five stages: opening, build-up, problem, action / resolution and ending. Ask the learners, in pairs, to collaboratively retell a well-known fable, for example 'The Tortoise and the Hare' by Aesop (you may have to read this to them first) and decide which parts of the story fit into which boxes. For example:

	The Tortoise and the Hare
Opening – introduce setting and characters	Tortoise and hare decide to have a race
Build-up – hint of a problem	Hare runs quickly, but decides to rest
Main part – a problem	Tortoise plods on, goes past sleeping hare
Action / resolution	Tortoise wins race
Ending	Moral – slow and steady wins the race

- Ask the learners to read the short traditional story on photocopiable page 57 (a Native American myth) and complete the task.

Top tips

- Create three large books in the class and encourage the learners to collect examples of fables, myths and legends. This will help them to identify the correct features but also provide a bank of ideas and structures that may then transfer into writing.
- Ask the learners to pick favourite stories and learn them in order to retell them to a younger audience. This will further embed the features and structures.

Study Guide

See pages 52–53 of the Study Guide for further work on boxing-up the parts of a story.

Name: _____

Fables, myths and legends

It was a hot day and OLD-man was trying to sleep, but the heat made him sick. He wandered to a hilltop for air; but there was no air. Then he went down to the river and found no relief. He travelled to the timberlands, and there the heat was great, although he found plenty of shade. The travelling made him warmer, of course, but he wouldn't stay still.

By and by he called to the winds to blow, and they began. First they didn't blow very hard, because they were afraid they might make OLD-man angry, but he kept crying:

'Blow harder – harder – harder! Blow worse than ever you blew before, and send this heat away from the world.'

So the winds did blow harder – harder than they ever had blown before.

'Bend and break, Fir-Tree!' cried OLD-man, and the Fir-Tree did bend and break. 'Bend and break, Pine-Tree!' and the Pine-Tree did bend and break. 'Bend and break, Spruce-Tree!' and the Spruce-Tree did bend and break. 'Bend and break, O Birch-Tree!' and the Birch-Tree did bend, but it wouldn't break.

'Ho! Birch-Tree, won't you mind me? Bend and break! I tell you,' but all the Birch-Tree would do was to bend. It bent to the ground; it bent double to please OLD-man, but it would not break.

'Blow harder, wind!' cried OLD-man, 'Blow harder and break the Birch-Tree.' The wind tried to blow harder, but it couldn't, and that made the thing worse, because OLD-man was so angry he went crazy. 'Break! I tell you – break!' screamed OLD-man at the Birch-Tree.

'I won't break,' replied the Birch. 'I shall never break for any wind. I will bend, but I shall never, never break.'

'You won't, hey?' cried OLD-man, and he rushed at the Birch-Tree with his hunting knife. He began slashing the bark of the Birch-Tree with the knife. All up and down the trunk of the tree OLD-man slashed, until the Birch was covered with the knife slashes.

'There! That is for not minding me. That will do you good! As long as time lasts you shall always look like that, Birch-Tree; always be marked as one who will not mind its maker. Yes, and all the Birch-Trees in the world shall have the same marks for ever.'

1 Is this a fable, a myth or a legend? _____

2 How do you know? 📄

3 Why do you think there was plenty of shade in the timberlands? 📄

4 Identify the parts of this simple traditional story by making notes in a table under the headings 'Opening' (introduce setting and characters), 'Build-up' (hint of a problem), 'Main part' (a problem), 'Action / resolution' and 'Ending'. 📄

Reading

Poetry – figurative language

Let's revise!

- Read the poem on photocopiable page 59 to the learners before giving them a copy. Model reading with expression with attention to the punctuation, and ask them to really listen to the descriptions and the vocabulary used. Give the learners two minutes to discuss what they have heard – first impressions, likes / dislikes and the images it creates. As a class, talk about the feedback.

- Ask the learners to re-read the poem on photocopiable page 59 and highlight or underline any vocabulary or phrases that really stand out. Ask them to feed back, or discuss with a partner, why these words and phrases particularly stand out for them. What images are created? Discuss why the poet has chosen these particular words and not others, for example: 'angry thunder', 'lighthouse of the sun'.

- Revise examples of figurative language by asking the learners to find them in the poem and repeating them out loud:
  - **alliteration** – 'white wave' (repetition of *w*)
  - **metaphor** – 'the lighthouse of the sun' (not *like* a lighthouse)
  - **personification** – 'They argue and quarrel'
  - **simile** – 'moods change like the weather'.

- Discuss the effect of this language. How does it make the learners feel when they read it?

- Ask the learners to complete the questions on photocopiable page 59, further exploring the poet's use of language.

- Make the poem come to life to enjoy the language! Put the learners into small groups and allow time for them to create a performance of the poem. They can present it in a variety of ways – as a choral piece, all speaking together; dividing it up into sections; adding movement, actions or sound effects; one acting as narrator while others add movement; adding music or displaying images during the performance.

Name: _____

Poetry – figurative language

Mountains

Mountains are today, yesterday, and for ever.

They have no likes or dislikes, no opinions, –

But moods, yes. Their moods change like the weather.

They argue and quarrel loud

With angry thunder. They rain

Rivers of stinging tears.

They hide their sulky heads in cloud

For days and days. Then suddenly, all smiles again,

One by one

Their magic cliffs stand clear

And brave, above a sea of white wave,

Under the lighthouse of the sun.

Ian Serraillier

The poet uses many features to bring the scene to life and paint a picture for the reader.

1 Explain what each of the following is and then draw a line to an example in the poem.

a Alliteration

_____

_____

b A metaphor

_____

_____

c Personification

_____

_____

d A simile

_____

_____

2 What do you think is happening when the mountains are 'arguing'?

_____

_____

3 What do you think the 'sea of white wave' might be?

_____

_____

_____

_____

4 Using alliteration, describe the sun in the last line.

The l_____ lighthouse of the s_____ sun.

5 Perform this poem with a group.

Reading

Play-scripts

Learning objectives

- Understand how expressive and descriptive language creates mood. (4Rf9)
- Read and perform play-scripts, exploring how scenes are built up. (4Rf12)
- Compare dialogue and dramatic conventions in film narrative. (5Rf11)
- Analyse the success of writing in evoking particular moods. (6Rf5)
- Articulate personal responses to reading, with close references to the text. (6Rf11)

Let's revise!

- Revise the features of play-scripts:
  - **purpose:** to entertain
  - **structure:** balance of background information, stage directions and dialogue
  - **features:** name of the character appears at the side of the page; dialogue is conversational and reflective of the character; stage directions and background information are often in a different type, in brackets; arranged in scenes.
- Ask the learners to discuss any plays they have seen or performed. Ask them to talk about some of their favourite characters and explain why they like or dislike them.
- Discuss the importance of actors building a character and making it come to life for the audience. The lines and the stage directions provide a starting point, but actors also draw on a number of other factors, such as personal feelings and previous experiences, people they have met, characters they have seen portrayed on TV or in films, and so on. Discuss how these connections can help to develop a more convincing character and therefore a more interesting scene.
- Read the extract from 'A night under the stars' by Stephanie Austwick on photocopiable page 61. Discuss the layout and the features with the learners, such as the stage directions, the characters' names, the use of italics. Draw their attention to the way the playwright has developed the atmosphere of the scene and the personality of the characters through both stage directions and dialogue. Then ask the learners to complete the revision questions, stating their own personal opinions.
- In pairs, play *First lines*. Give the learners a first line that could belong to one of the characters in the extract, for example: 'But I'm scared!' Ask them to continue the conversation this character might have with one of the other characters. Allow time for the learners to perform their scenes, and write or improvise more if they wish.

Top tips

To explore and develop a character, create a 'role on the wall' for the character. On a large sheet of paper, write down everything the learners know or can imagine about the character: their background, their likes and dislikes, their feelings, the way they speak, what they might wear, how they might move, and so on. Try hot-seating the characters to explore them further.

Study Guide

See pages 56–57 of the Study Guide for further exploration of characters in play-scripts.

Name: _____

Play-scripts

Jack, Roul, Brad and Lex are sitting outside their tents in a small clearing. It is almost 10 o'clock at night, the darkness has closed in around them and the fire is just a pile of smouldering embers. Jack shivers.

Jack: (*grumpily*) I've had enough. Let's go to bed. It's getting late and I'm frozen.

Roul: (*pulling his blanket around him*) Could do. I think we should build up the fire first. It'll keep us warm and keep the wild animals away.

Lex: (*sitting up suddenly*) What wild animals? You didn't say there would be wild animals!

Roul: We're in the middle of a forest. Of course there's going to be wild animals!

Lex begins to look around nervously.

Brad: It's OK – he means things like rabbits and mice and stuff.

Jack: There isn't any more wood. Someone will have to go and find some.

Lex: (*nervously*) Well, I'm not going. It's pitch black out there. And I thought I heard something move.

Roul: (*leaning towards Lex, whispering*) It's probably a man-eating wolf or a grizzly bear. Maybe it's that black beast that's been spotted roaming through the countryside! I read about it in the paper.

Brad: Stop teasing him, Roul – he's only young.

Jack: (*getting up*) Look – I don't care what you lot are doing. I'm going to bed. It's going to be warmer in my sleeping bag.

Jack shuffles off to bed, still muttering and grumbling under his breath.

An owl screeches overhead – making them all jump – even Roul!

1 What do we know about the setting? _____

2 What do we know about the character of each boy?

_____

_____

_____

3 How do the stage directions help the actors to develop the characters?

_____

_____

4 What happens next? Write the next six lines of the script.

5 Perform the scene so far.

Reading

Autobiographies and biographies

Learning objectives

- Explore the features of texts which are about events and experiences. (5Rn6)
- Explore autobiography and biography, and first and third person narration. (6Rn3)

Let's revise!

- Revise the features of autobiographies and biographies (recounts):
  - **purpose** of both: to inform or entertain – a recount of events in the life of someone, or a description of that person's life
  - **features** of both: often past tense (but may include present and future), usually chronological
  - feature of autobiography: told in the first person (*I did something*)
  - feature of biography: told in the third person (*he / she did something*).
- Have a few examples for the learners to look at – books about real sports people, scientists, artists; diaries; theatre programmes that include biographies; websites, and so on.
- Ask the learners to think of three things that they did when they were younger. They should then swap these facts with a partner. Choose a few volunteers to stand up and tell the class about their partner. Discuss the difference between describing yourself and what *you* have done (autobiography) and talking about someone else's life (biography).
- Revise the use of first and third person and the past tense. Ask the learners to think about when it may be necessary to include facts in the present or future tense.
- Revise the fact that, although we refer to autobiographies and biographies as non-fiction texts – someone is recounting the actual facts of a life story (either their own, or that of someone else) – there is also autobiographical / biographical style in fiction. Here the features are exactly the same; although the content may not be based on a real life, it is written as if it is. Many authors employ this style. (See the example on photocopiable page 63.)
- Explore a selection of fiction and non-fiction texts. Ask the learners to decide which are biographies and which are autobiographies / which are written in an autobiographical or biographical style. Discuss the fact that some famous celebrities employ ghost writers to write their 'autobiographies' for them!
- Ask the learners to read the two texts on photocopiable page 63 and answer the accompanying questions.

Top tips

The features of biographies and autobiographies are quite easy to identify, but learners often find it difficult to remember which one is which. A simple mnemonic or a visual representation can sometimes help but these are often more effective if composed by the learner. For example, I **auto**matically talk about myself because that's what I know best! Therefore it is **auto**biography.

Study Guide

See pages 58–61 of the Study Guide for further examples of biographies and autobiographies.

Name: _____

Autobiographies and biographies

Autobiographical style

From a very early age, I was aware of the existence of dragons, but I soon realised that not everyone was lucky enough to be able to see them. At first, I tried to point them out to people – my parents, my sister, the other children in my class – but they just laughed. My grandfather and I, though, would spend many hours at the bottom of his garden, just watching them.

Every spring, the eggs would hatch and we would delight in seeing the baby dragonlets learn to fly. Sometimes, they would get a bit overenthusiastic during fire-breathing lessons, so Grandpa had to keep a fire extinguisher handy!

I was always sad when the time came for the young dragons to leave. They would stretch their tiny, iridescent wings and float gracefully away.

Biographical style

When Kezia Jones was a child, she believed in dragons. Imagine. Not Komodo dragons or anything like that. She believed in fire-breathing, flying, magical dragons! Apparently, they lived at the bottom of her grandpa's garden.

Often, on a Monday morning, she would tell the other children about how she had spent the weekend watching the young dragons as they learnt to fly or how her grandpa had used the fire extinguisher because an overexcited dragonlet had set fire to the bushes. She would get really excited when the eggs hatched but upset again when they flew away.

1 What is the difference between the two styles?

_____

_____

2 How do you think the author of the autobiography feels about the dragons? Give reasons for your answer.

_____

_____

3 Do you think the author of the biography believes in the dragons? Give reasons for your answer.

_____

4 Write your own autobiography or a biography of a friend, a relative or your pet.

Reading

Persuasion

Learning objectives

- Investigate how persuasive writing is used to convince a reader and note the use of persuasive devices, words and phrases in print and other media. (4Rn5, 5Rn5)
- Compare writing that informs and persuades. (5Rn9)
- Analyse how paragraphs are structured and linked. (6Rn1)
- Establish and maintain a clear viewpoint, with some elaboration of personal voice. (6Wf3)
- Argue a case in writing, developing points logically and convincingly. (6Wn6)

Let's revise!

- Revise the features of persuasive texts:
  - **purpose:** to argue the case for a point of view; to attempt to convince the reader
  - **structure:** opening statement; arguments to persuade with elaboration; summary and closing statement
  - **features:** present tense; logical connectives, for example because, however; time connectives, for example firstly, finally; strong, positive language; facts to back up the arguments; appropriate use of questions; may include exaggeration.

- Give learners, in groups, ten minutes to prepare a short presentation to persuade you to do something, for example hold a school disco, allow them to have mobile phones on their desks, turn the hall into an indoor swimming pool. It can be more interesting if each group chooses something different and if it is something they can really identify with. They should prepare their arguments, elaborate on the reasons behind their request, choose their persuasive language carefully for maximum effect and decide how they will present it to you. Then hear each presentation. Discuss:
  - the language used, considering what was effective and why, and from this, make a class list for reference
  - the structure of the presentations: an introduction, a main point with reasons, a second point with reasons, and so on
  - the importance of grouping the information in an organised way – not jumping from one reason to another and then back again.

- As a class, read a range of appropriate persuasive texts, such as adverts in papers, fliers, packaging, making a note of the persuasive words and phrases used. Discuss which texts are the most effective. Where possible, find examples with the points grouped in paragraphs.

- To revise the use of persuasive devices and language, ask the learners to read the text on photocopiable page 65 and answer the questions.

Top tips

When studying persuasive writing, give the learners opportunities to write for a real audience and purpose as this will add weight to the task. They will use more emotive language and produce stronger persuasive arguments if the subject is important to them, for example: write a letter to local residents persuading them to take care of the environment; help to create a play area; or visit an exhibition created by the learners in school.

Study Guide

See pages 62–63 of the Study Guide for further work on persuasive writing.

Name: _____

Persuasion

Pod 3403

Dear Space Agent 491,

With reference to your advertisement in *The Intergalactic Traveller*, I would like to be considered for the once in a lifetime mission – Patrol to Planet Earth.

Firstly, from a very early age, it has been a burning ambition of mine to travel through the galaxy and I have spent several thousand eons studying the possibility of life on Earth. I am, without doubt, the leading galactic expert on primitive life forces and I truly believe that there is no other agent who can rival my knowledge.

Furthermore, I am extremely good at working as part of a team and I have had a great deal of experience of living in confined spaces for long periods of time.

Finally, I am fanatically fearless and would not be intimidated by the primitive life forms we may encounter on Planet Earth.

I hope that you will consider my application and I await your reply with anticipation.

Yours faithfully

SP 609

1 How had the author of this letter heard about the mission?

_____

2 What had SP 609 spent thousands of eons doing?

_____

3 Circle three connectives used within this letter.

4 Pick three reasons the writer gives that would make him the right person for this mission.

_____

_____

_____

5 Suggest some alternative persuasive phrases the author could have used instead of the following:

extremely good _____

great deal (of experience) _____

Reading

Discussion

Learning objectives

- Understand how points are ordered to make a coherent argument. (4Rn1)
- Compare and evaluate the print and film versions of a novel or play. (5Rf10)
- Read and evaluate non-fiction texts for purpose, style, clarity and organisation. (5Rn8)
- Use connectives to structure an argument or discussion. (6GPw3)
- Identify features of balanced written arguments. (6Rn4)
- Write a balanced report of a controversial issue. (6Wn7)

Let's revise!

- Revise the features of discussion texts:
  - **purpose:** to present arguments and information from differing viewpoints
  - **structure:** introductory statement; arguments on one side, counter-arguments; summary
  - **features:** present tense; logical connectives, for example however, therefore; sequential connectives where appropriate, for example firstly, finally; questions where appropriate; elaboration on both sides of the argument; summary plus a recommendation if appropriate.

- Create a scenario to practise and revise discussion (and persuasion) skills. For example, tell the class that you're not sleeping very well. You are going to decorate your bedroom and you are thinking of painting it black. Divide the group in half. One side must think of reasons why black would be a great colour for a bedroom; the other side must think of reasons why it would not. (They must ignore what they actually believe.) Allow the groups five minutes to talk. Encourage the learners to back up their arguments with powerful elaboration, such as 'a black room might feel like a cave and you may feel as if you have been trapped underground'. Hear the arguments on both sides, alternating the contributions. Having heard the information on both sides, have a secret vote and see whether black wins. Discuss the importance of weighing up both sides of the argument and the language and style used to present both sides.

- The above activity can also be done by giving a discussion topic to groups of learners, such as: 'Which is better – snow or sun?', 'Who should be king of the jungle – a lion or an elephant?' or 'Where would you like to visit – a beach or a forest?', or more thought-provoking topics such as: 'Is it right to keep animals in zoos?' or 'Is it ever right to test drugs on animals?'

- Ask each group to work together to present the facts on both sides to the rest of the class and then have a vote. Encourage them to use logical connectives when presenting the facts, for example: however, as a result of this, therefore; and sequential connectives where appropriate, for example: firstly, finally.

- Reflect on the presentations and discuss the need for balanced arguments when giving people a choice.

- Ask the learners to read the discussion text on photocopiable page 67, discuss the features and answer the questions. Explain that in some discussion texts there may be more than two options for the reader to choose from. The process of grouping the information and presenting the facts is exactly the same.

Top tips

When presenting the facts in a discussion text it is important to group the information appropriately. Some discussion texts are more effective if a point is made and immediately followed by its counter-argument, whereas other discussion texts work better if all the facts on one side are presented together, followed by all the facts on the other side. Ask the learners which they prefer.

Study Guide

See pages 64–65 of the Study Guide for more work on discussion texts.

Name: _____

Discussion

> **The Creature Contraption**
>
> Breaking news: Scientists have created 'The Creature Contraption' – a machine that can give you the abilities of any creature for just one day. All you need to do is decide whether you want to be a creature on land, in the sea or in the air.
>
> Firstly, land creatures. Some might say this is the safer, less exciting option, but think again. You could be climbing vertically up the side of the tallest building, leaping over obstacles or racing across the plains as fast as the wind. Imagine doing that for a day.
>
> On the other hand, you may feel that as we already spend most of our time on land it would be better to do something completely different. You might choose to have the ability to glide gracefully down a gently flowing river, spiral and leap through the mighty waves, or swim amongst the coral in turquoise, tropical waters.
>
> Finally, consider how would it feel to be up in the air, looking down on the Earth. Man has always longed to fly, not just in aeroplanes but swooping and diving on the jet streams, exploring the world, as free as a bird!
>
> All three options sound exciting. Which one will you choose?

1 What do you notice about how the paragraphs are organised in this text?

_____

_____

2 List three reasons, stated in the text, for choosing the abilities of a land creature.

_____

_____

_____

3 Why is it important for the author to present all three options equally?

_____

_____

4 If you had a choice, would you want to be a creature on the land, in the sea or in the air? Give three reasons for your decision.

_____

_____

_____

_____

Reading

Instructions

Let's revise!

- Revise the key features of instructional texts:
  - **purpose:** to instruct, using a series of sequenced steps
  - **structure:** title – stating the goal; materials / equipment needed; series of sequenced steps; sometimes diagrams or illustrations
  - **features:** use of the imperative form, for example: sift the flour; numbered, lettered or bullet points and sequential language to indicate order; short, clear sentences, making the instruction sound easy; extra information added to help the reader when appropriate.

- Play the *Add an action* game to revise the imperative form. Begin by giving the learners a set of three instructions that require actions, for example stand on one leg; rub you tummy; hop three times. They must perform these actions in the order they were given. Then ask a learner to repeat the instructions and add one of their own. The learners must perform them all again, and so on. (Remember, there needs to be an instruction to put the leg down at some point!) Ask the learners to write down some of the instructions, underlining the imperative verb. This activity could be adapted further to include sequential language – sentences must be repeated exactly as they were given and no two consecutive sentences can begin in the same way, for example: First ..., next ..., after that ..., then ..., subsequently ...

- To revise the layout and language features of instructions in a memorable and amusing way, read the unappetising-sounding recipe on photocopiable page 69 and discuss. Ask the learners to underline the key features, for example headings and imperative verbs. Discuss the range of verbs used and then ask the learners to answer the questions.

Top tips

A short, practical, fun game, such as *Simon says*, often helps the language features to stick in the mind of the learners better than copious written examples. One learner delivers instructions to the others. If the instruction begins with 'Simon says' (for example: 'Simon says touch your nose'), the learners should do it; if it doesn't, they should not carry out the instruction. If they get it wrong, they must sit down. The winner is the one who is left standing.

Study Guide

See pages 66–67 of the Study Guide for further work on instructional writing.

Name: _____

Instructions

Frightful Fantasy Fizz for Funny Folk (Don't try this at home!)

You will need:

Equipment

A large, flameproof cooking pot   A wooden mixing spoon

6 goblets

Ingredients

2 cups of murky ditchwater   1 cup of mouldy mushrooms

½ cup of sour milk   200 grams of mixed weeds

2 squirts of shampoo   4 pairs of smelly socks

1 teaspoon of fresh cabbage juice

Method

1 Gather all your equipment and ingredients together but DO NOT WASH YOUR HANDS!

2 Pour the ditchwater, mushrooms and sour milk into the cooking pot.

3 Add the mixed weeds, a few clumps at a time, and stir in gently with the wooden spoon.

4 Carefully squirt in the shampoo, making sure the mixture does not splash over the sides.

5 Gently place the smelly socks into the centre of the mixture, one at a time. You may notice a slight fizzing as they dissolve – this is quite normal.

6 Finally, add the cabbage juice, mix until the desired level of lumpiness is achieved and pour into goblets to serve.

1 Why is the title so important? _____

2 Why do you think the writer used capital letters in step 1?

_____

3 How does the way this recipe is set out help the reader?

_____

4 What would happen if the steps were not in sequence?

_____

5 Rewrite steps 1–6, replacing the numbers with sequential language, such as: first, finally, next, before you start, then, after that.

Reading

Explanations

Learning objectives

- Understand how paragraphs and chapters are used to organise ideas. (4Rn2)
- Understand the use of impersonal style in explanatory texts. (5Rn7)
- Compare the language, style and impact of a range of non-fiction writing. (6Rn5)

Let's revise!

- Revise the features of explanation texts:
  - **purpose:** to explain the processes involved in achieving something; to explain how something works or why something happens
  - **structure:** general statement to introduce topic; series of logical points explaining how or why; closing statement, relating to the reader when possible
  - **features:** simple present tense; causal connectives, such as: because, so, therefore, if (this is done) then ..., as a result of; time connectives, such as: firstly, secondly, next, finally; impersonal style.
- Make class lists of time and causal connectives and connecting phrases.
- Ask the learners, in pairs, to explain to each other why it is important to learn to read. At this stage, do not stress the impersonal style. Many may begin by addressing the listener directly – 'You need to learn to read because ...'
- Revise the use of the impersonal style – the explanation is informing the reader but not appealing to 'you' directly as in instructions. For example: 'You should learn to read because ...' becomes 'It is important to learn to read because ...' or 'By learning to read it is possible to ...' or 'If a person becomes good at reading ...' Ask the learners to repeat the above exercise of explaining something to their partner but using the impersonal style.
- Read the text on photocopiable page 71 as a class. Ask the learners to pick out phrases that emphasise the impersonal style, for example: 'it is possible to', 'this should not be used'. They should then complete the activity on the sheet.

Top tips

It is useful to compare sets of instructions and explanations as these often get confused. To do this, display a clear list of features side by side and talk about the differences.

Study Guide

See pages 68–69 of the Study Guide for further revision of explanation texts.

Name: _____

Explanations

How to avoid the washing up on a regular basis!

Most people like to avoid doing the washing up from time to time. However, it is possible to do this on a regular basis, by following a few simple tips.

First, the magical words 'I need to make a start on my homework' can work wonders. Warning – do not use too often as this may arouse suspicion!

Next, some parents can be very easily diverted, so offering to fetch something from the local shop or the neighbour's house is sometimes all that is needed to ensure a stroll through the park in the sunshine, instead of an hour standing next to a sink.

However, if it is cold outside, another way of avoiding those suds is to suddenly develop a minor illness, perhaps a headache, earache or toothache. It is important that it should not be seen to be too serious so that parents do not become overly worried, and it needs to allow for a rapid recovery once the washing up is done. Beware – this method is not fool-proof as believability is often a factor. If the acting is not of a good standard, the plan will fail.

Finally, the most effective way to avoid washing-up duties is to encourage adults to invest in a machine that will perform this odious task. Alternatively, a person could be employed who will do the job on a regular basis. This might take all the fun out of the task avoidance exercise, but may provide a very welcome ally for many years to come.

1 What is this explanation helping the reader to achieve? _____

_____

2 Why is the text split up into paragraphs? _____

3 Give a short title to each of the paragraphs.   **1** _____

    2 _____   **3** _____

    4 _____   **5** _____

4 Try reading this passage, putting it into the past tense. Why do you think the present tense is used for explanations?

_____

5 Write a short explanation text on a subject of your choice, for example:
- How to become an expert in …
- Why friends are important
- Why it is vital to get enough sleep.

Reading

Recounts

Learning objectives

- Identify different types of non-fiction text and recognise their key characteristics. (4Rn3, 6Rn2)
- Read newspaper reports and consider how they engage the reader. (4Rn4)
- Explore the features of texts which are about events and experiences, e.g. diaries. (5Rn6)

Let's revise!

- Revise the features of a recount:
  - **purpose:** to retell events
  - **structure:** opening statement or paragraph; events as they occurred; closing statement
  - **features:** past tense; chronological order; time connectives, for example: first, later, after; details to bring events to life (may be exaggerated!); specific names, places; direct quotes, when appropriate; sometimes written in a way that encourages empathy from the reader.

- Ask the learners, in pairs, to recount their journey to school to each other, from leaving the house to entering the classroom. Discuss the use of the past tense, the chronology and the importance of the little details.

- Look at a number of different recounts, for example a newspaper report, a diary entry, a biography – anything that retells a sequence of events.

- Revise the purpose, structure and features (see above), but remind the learners that it is also possible to have a recount with fictional content. Once the learners understand the structure and language of a recount, these can be applied to writing about a school trip they have just been on or the events in a favourite story. Discuss the fact that the viewpoint of the author is often obvious in the writing.

- Ask the learners to write down their journey to school, including the features discussed, for example: I trudged slowly, my bag getting heavier with every step.

- Explain that most newspaper *reports* are in fact recounts – they tell about something that has happened. Discuss the fact that the way a recount is written can sometimes serve other purposes, such as to persuade or influence the reader. To illustrate this, try reading about the same incident in two different newspapers.

- Ask the learners to complete the exercise based on the recount of the series of events in 'Goldilocks and the Three Bears' on photocopiable page 73.

Top tips

It is always advisable to ask the learners to write from their own experience when producing recounts. This enables them to relive the events, add in the details, and so on. However, if this is not possible, writing recounts of events in stories, and so on, can provide a fun way to practise the skills.

Study Guide

See pages 70–71 of the Study Guide for a further example of a recount.

Recounts

> **BREAKING NEWS!**
>
> ## SERIAL INTRUDER STRIKES AGAIN! IS ANY HOME SAFE?
>
> Yesterday, the sleepy village of Bearswood was rocked by the news that a cottage, belonging to Mr and Mrs Brown and their son Barney, aged 10, had been ransacked by a notorious local youth.
>
> First, the intruder, a young female who cannot be named due to her age, entered the dwelling through the front door, which the owners admitted to having left unlocked while they went for their early morning stroll.
>
> She then proceeded to eat their food and destroy their furniture, before falling asleep in young Barney's bed – a bed that should represent a warm, cosy, safe place to be, but may never feel the same again for this poor, innocent creature.
>
> Sometime later, on returning home and discovering the damage, Mr Brown chased the intruder out of the building. She was then apprehended by the local police.
>
> 'This is not the first time we have had dealings with this young lady,' said Chief Inspector B B Wolf. 'She has had a number of warnings in the past but does not seem to have learnt her lesson. We will be taking this latest incident very seriously.'
>
> The trial will begin on Monday.

1 How does the headline grab the readers and make them want to read on? _____

_____

_____

2 This is a recount. What tense is it written in and why? _____

_____

3 Why can't the intruder be named in this newspaper report? _____

_____

4 What time connectives has the writer used? _____

_____

5 Why do newspaper reporters use direct quotes? _____

_____

_____

6 Write the same report as if you are on the side of the poor little girl with no food and nowhere to stay. 📝

Reading

Reports

- Identify different types of non-fiction text and recognise their key characteristics. (4Rn3, 6Rn2)
- Look for information in non-fiction texts to build on what is already known. (5Rn1)

Let's revise!

- Revise the features of non-chronological reports:
  - **purpose:** to give information
  - **structure:** an opening statement or introduction; a range of information, arranged in sections
  - **features:** present tense; non-chronological; often moves from general to specific, for example from occupations in general to sections on teachers, doctors, actors.
- Ask the learners, in pairs, to prepare a five-minute talk about something they are interested in, such as horses, football or space. Ensure they consider the features of a non-chronological report. Their notes should just consist of a series of headings and subheadings and they should then talk from their own knowledge.
- Hear some of these talks and discuss the organisation of the information. Ask questions such as: Why is it important not to jump around from one area to another and back again? Does it matter in which order you introduce the sections? Must you talk about feeding your horse before you mention riding it? Why does it help to add extra bits of detail?
- Look at a range of information books that use headings and subheadings to organise the text. Discuss how this helps the reader.
- Ask the learners to complete the revision activities on photocopiable page 75.
- Ask them to think of something they are really interested in, and then decide how they would split up the information. They should draw some boxes like the ones on photocopiable page 75 and then write the headings and any brief notes in them.

Top tips

Explain to the learners that when planning a non-chronological report, it is often helpful to write each section on a sticky note, or small piece of paper, and then physically move the sections around the page before deciding where they should go in the final draft.

Study Guide

See pages 72–73 of the Study Guide for further revision of non-chronological reports.

Reports

The Tomb of Tutankhamen

The discovery

In 1922, the famous archaeologist Howard Carter discovered the lost tomb of the Egyptian boy king Tutankhamen in the Valley of the Kings in Egypt.

The tomb

The tomb consisted of an antechamber, a burial chamber, an annex and a treasure chamber.

Treasures of the tomb

King Tut's tomb was the most complete tomb of an Egyptian king ever discovered.

The custom was to bury the kings with everything they would need for their journey to the afterlife.

Objects found in this tomb included a solid-gold death mask, mummified pets and even some strips of cloth for the king to use as toilet paper!

The Mummy's Curse

There are lots of superstitions surrounding the opening of these tombs. Some believe that there is magic guarding them and those who disturb them will suffer the Mummy's Curse!

Did you know?

The scorpion was thought to be the embodiment of the Mummy's Curse.

1 What have you learnt about the discovery of the tomb? _____

_____

_____

2 What objects were found in the tomb? _____

_____

_____

3 How did the organisation of the information help you to locate the facts?

_____

_____

4 Do these boxes have to be read in a certain order? Give a reason for your answer.

_____

_____

Quick quiz 3

> ### Francis Barber
>
> Francis Barber was born in Jamaica and was brought to England in 1750 by a Captain Bathurst. Francis was sent to school at Barton in Yorkshire. Capt. Bathurst died in 1752 and gave Francis his freedom.
>
> Francis then became a servant to Dr Samuel Johnson, a friend of the Bathurst family. Dr Johnson is most famous as the man who made the first English dictionary. Dr Johnson sent Francis to school at Bishops Stortford, Hertfordshire. Francis Barber lived with him in his house off Fleet Street, and also at Streatham Place in South London, for many years.
>
> When Dr Johnson died in 1782, Francis was left his property, an income of £70 a year and all his books and personal possessions. Francis then moved to Lichfield with his wife, Elizabeth, whom he married in 1776. They ran a school at Burntwood, near Lichfield, until Francis became ill. He died in January 1801 at Stafford Infirmary. Elizabeth Barber carried on teaching for another fifteen years.
>
> Elizabeth and Francis Barber had four children. One of them, Samuel, was a Methodist minister and one grandson emigrated to the United States. Another continued to live in the Staffordshire area.
>
> *(From a history textbook written by two teachers at Tulse Hill School, in South London)*

1 Tick (✓) **one** box. This entry is:

   a biography ☐   an autobiography ☐   an instruction ☐   [1]

2 What does it mean that Bathurst 'gave Francis his freedom'?

   _____

   _____

   _____   [1]

3 What is Dr Johnson most famous for?

   _____

   _____

   _____   [1]

 Revise for Cambridge Primary Checkpoint English Teacher's Guide © Hodder & Stoughton Ltd 2013

Name: _____

4 According to these dates, for how many years did Francis live under the care and guidance of Dr Johnson?

_____ [1]

5 Why do you think Dr Johnson left everything to Francis when he died?

_____

_____ [1]

6 What jobs did Francis and Elizabeth take on afterwards?

_____

_____ [1]

7 What did they call one of their sons and why?

_____

_____

_____ [1]

8 There are four paragraphs in this extract, each covering a different part of Francis' life. Give a title to each paragraph.

a _____ [1]

b _____ [1]

c _____ [1]

d _____ [1]

9 There is no description in this piece. Why is this?

_____

_____ [1]

10 Do you think Captain Bathurst was a kind man? Give reasons for your answer.

_____

_____

_____

_____

_____

_____ [2]

Quick quiz 3 answers

> **Francis Barber**
>
> Francis Barber was born in Jamaica and was brought to England in 1750 by a Captain Bathurst. Francis was sent to school at Barton in Yorkshire. Capt. Bathurst died in 1752 and gave Francis his freedom.
>
> Francis then became a servant to Dr Samuel Johnson, a friend of the Bathurst family. Dr Johnson is most famous as the man who made the first English dictionary. Dr Johnson sent Francis to school at Bishops Stortford, Hertfordshire. Francis Barber lived with him in his house off Fleet Street, and also at Streatham Place in South London, for many years.
>
> When Dr Johnson died in 1782, Francis was left his property, an income of £70 a year and all his books and personal possessions. Francis then moved to Lichfield with his wife, Elizabeth, whom he married in 1776. They ran a school at Burntwood, near Lichfield, until Francis became ill. He died in January 1801 at Stafford Infirmary. Elizabeth Barber carried on teaching for another fifteen years.
>
> Elizabeth and Francis Barber had four children. One of them, Samuel, was a Methodist minister and one grandson emigrated to the United States. Another continued to live in the Staffordshire area.
>
> *(From a history textbook written by two teachers at Tulse Hill School, in South London)*

1 Tick (✓) **one** box. This entry is:

   a biography ✓   an autobiography ☐   an instruction ☐   [1]

2 What does it mean that Bathurst 'gave Francis his freedom'?

   Francis must have been a slave in Jamaica and he was set free.   [1]

3 What is Dr Johnson most famous for?

   Dr Johnson made the first English dictionary.   [1]

Revise for Cambridge Primary Checkpoint English Teacher's Guide © Hodder & Stoughton Ltd 2013

4 According to these dates, for how many years did Francis live under the care and guidance of Dr Johnson?

Francis lived with Johnson for thirty years. [1]

5 Why do you think Dr Johnson left everything to Francis when he died?

He must have been very fond of Francis and perhaps he did not

have any family of his own. [1]

6 What jobs did Francis and Elizabeth take on afterwards?

They became teachers and ran a school. [1]

7 What did they call one of their sons and why?

They called one of their sons Samuel. They named him after

Dr Johnson because he had been good to them. [1]

8 There are four paragraphs in this extract, each covering a different part of Francis' life. Give a title to each paragraph.

For example:

a **Introduction or background to Francis Barber** [1]

b **Life with Dr Johnson** [1]

c **His work and his death** [1]

d **His family** [1]

9 There is no description in this piece. Why is this?

There is no description because it is a factual piece of information. [1]

10 Do you think Captain Bathurst was a kind man? Give reasons for your answer.

For example:

I think Captain Bathurst was kind because he rescued Francis

from slavery; he looked after Francis; he sent Francis to school;

he arranged for Francis to live with Dr Johnson. [2]

Writing

Planning stories

- Explore different ways of planning stories, and write longer stories from plans. (4Wf1)
- Map out writing to plan structure, e.g. paragraphs, sections, chapters. (5Wf1)
- Plan plot, characters and structure effectively in writing an extended story. (6Wf1)

Let's revise!

- Revise the different formats learners might use when planning a story:
  - **notes**
  - **storyboards:** a series of boxes, rather like a comic strip, with key information in each
  - **story mountains:** a simple mountain shape with key information written at each point – beginning, build-up, climax, resolution, ending
  - **story maps:** a simple journey mapped out on a page, with key information at each stage of the story.
- Each of these generally covers the five main parts of a story:
  - opening
  - build-up
  - problem
  - action or resolution
  - ending.

  Use a well-known story to demonstrate and revise each of these parts.
- If the learners already have an idea in mind, any of the above formats work well but it is important to remind them that writers should try not to put too much information into the plan. It is a structure to keep them on track, with a few key words or details.
- If writers struggle for an idea or find it hard to remember a structure, 'boxing up' is a technique that can be very supportive. Show the learners how to do this, using the plan on photocopiable page 81. First, take a well-known, easy-to-remember story with a simple structure, for example 'Goldilocks and the Three Bears'. Show the learners that the story has been split up into five parts. Demonstrate how to create the generic column in the middle by asking: 'What happens in this part?' and show how to create new ideas for the final column. Then ask the learners to fill in the empty boxes in the final column in order to plan a new story.
- Give the learners an opportunity to plan their new story in another format, such as a story mountain or a storyboard. Ask them which format they prefer.

Name: _____

Planning stories

	'Goldilocks and the Three Bears'	Generic model	Plan for new story
Opening	Three Bears Cottage in wood Make porridge – too hot Decide to go for a walk Leave the door open	Introduce character(s) Introduce setting Normal day Character(s) leave setting	New family move into house next door
Build-up	Goldilocks Walking in wood Finds cottage Enters cottage	New character (NC) introduced Enters setting	
Problem	Goldilocks explores cottage Breaks Little Bear's chair Eats Little Bear's porridge Falls asleep in Little Bear's bed	NC explores setting Causes a problem Stays in setting for some reason	
Action / resolution	Three Bears come home Discover chair Discover porridge Discover Goldilocks in bed		Family come back unexpectedly
Ending	Goldilocks wakes up Jumps out of the window and runs away		

1 Complete the 'generic model' column by considering what happens in 'Goldilocks and the Three Bears'.

2 Fill in the empty boxes in the final column to plan a new story.

3 Try writing the new story that you have planned. 🗒

4 Divide up other stories that you know into a table like the one above. This will give you lots of ideas for new stories. 🗒

Writing

Openings and endings

Let's revise!

- Discuss any stories the learners have read that have a great opening that made them want to read on. Read a few examples to the class. (This could also apply to films they have seen.) Discuss the features of a good opening – what should it do?

- Read the opening by Stephanie Austwick on photocopiable page 83. Discuss the purpose of this opening – introducing the character and the setting. Discuss the viewpoint of the character – it seems to be a favourite place, peaceful. Discuss the atmosphere that is created in the first paragraph – calm, peaceful, tranquil. Show some images of riverbanks, or play some atmospheric music to stimulate thoughts. Collect a list of good descriptive words and phrases for this setting. Discuss the change in atmosphere the writer is trying to create in the second paragraph – suspense, a hint of a problem. Explore how this is done – short sentences, choice of vocabulary.

- Ask the learners to retell the opening from photocopiable page 83 in their own words, as if it were happening to them. Encourage them to embellish it as much as they wish, putting in their own descriptions to make the scene come to life and hook the reader in. Allow time for the learners to complete tasks 1 and 2 on photocopiable page 83.

- Read the ending by Stephanie Austwick on page 83. Ask the learners to point out anything they notice, such as links with the opening and with what must have happened in the middle of the story. Ask them to consider what a good ending should do. Allow the learners time to complete the final activities on page 83.

Name: _____

Openings and endings

Opening

The moonlight was just beginning to shimmer on the surface of the water as Joe stepped onto the bridge. He paused for a while, watching a family of ducks as they splashed their way towards the riverbank for their nightly roost. Silently, he turned and made his way towards the water's edge, where he sat down under the bridge to watch the shadows dance among the ripples. It was so peaceful.

Suddenly, Joe was aware of a low rumbling sound. He thought he felt the ground shudder beneath him but that was impossible. He sat very still. Listening. Waiting. Silence. Then, as he held his breath, there it was again. The rumbling sound. The strange movement. What could it be? All at once Joe felt a swirling, furling, falling feeling and the ground began to swallow him up. He seemed to be enveloped in a thickening mist.

---

1 Using this example as a model, write the opening two paragraphs of your own adventure story. Introduce your character and your setting, taking care to add description.

2 Read what you have written to a partner. Does it make them want to hear what happens next?

Ending

Joe took the ruby-red leaf, the white feather and the smooth, black pebble out of his pocket and, holding all three objects in his right hand, uttered the words he had been instructed to say in order to leave this strange world. 'Rommily Round, homeward bound.' With a swirling, curling, furling feeling, Joe found himself once again in the middle of a strange mist.

Cautiously, he opened his eyes and there was the bridge rising above him, and the riverbank, and the family of ducks, as if he had never been away. But he had! Because there in his hand was a ruby-red leaf, a smooth black pebble and the whitest feather he had ever seen.

---

3 Write the ending for your own adventure story, making sure you link it to your ideas for the beginning.

4 Discuss with a partner what might have happened in the middle of the original story.

5 Write a brief plan for what could happen in the middle of your story.

Writing

Settings and characters

Learning objectives

- Write character profiles, using detail to capture the reader's imagination. (4Wf3)
- Use imagery and figurative language to evoke imaginative responses. (5Wf8)
- Use different genres as models for writing. (6Wf4)
- Plan plot, characters and structure effectively in writing an extended story. (6Wf1)

Let's revise!

- To revise the importance of creating an interesting setting for a story, show interesting images of forests, palaces, houses, cities, islands, caves, and so on. Great examples can be found on the internet. Alternatively, show film clips that include interesting, beautiful or atmospheric settings.

- Discuss the vocabulary that can be used to describe settings, such as figurative language, similes, metaphors, alliteration. Build a bank of ideas on the wall. See page 58 for further revision activities on similes, metaphors and alliteration.

- Read some extracts from exciting or interesting descriptions of settings or characters and ask the learners to discuss why the settings or characters are easy to visualise.

- Read the extract on photocopiable page 85 and discuss the image it creates. Ask the learners how the author does this. Discuss the use of more than one sense, and the personification of the building 'leaning'. Ask the learners to write the next paragraph, further describing the setting. Then ask them to continue by creating an equally sinister character who appears on the scene.

- Hear some of these descriptions and discuss if the learners have added details that bring the settings and characters to life for the audience.

Top tips

Visiting interesting settings, such as palaces, forests and beaches, is the best way to develop language. However, if these opportunities are not available, watch film clips, study images, listen to music such as *Night on the Bare Mountain* (1867) by Modest Mussorgsky, paint settings or read quality extracts. Encourage the learners to keep a note of any great ideas and powerful vocabulary.

Study Guide

Pages 82–83 of the Study Guide contain further examples of settings and characters and more opportunities to write.

Name: _____

Settings and characters

Setting

In the murkiest, slimiest, darkest corner of the East End, there was a crumbling old warehouse that even the rats had deserted. One side of it leaned crazily out over the river, and the other side leaned gloomily over the street.

It was called TURNER AND LUCKETT'S MEDICINAL SARSAPARILLA WAREHOUSE but there had been no sarsaparilla stored there for years. People believed it was haunted. Mysterious lights used to gleam behind the broken windows high up on the top floor, and hideous noises came filtering out over the rooftops in the middle of the night.

(from *Spring-Heeled Jack* by Philip Pullman)

1 Write the next paragraph, continuing to describe this spooky scene. Here are some words and phrases that may help: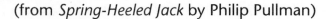

musty smell	creaking doors	broken hinges	rusty bars	moonlit street
piercing shrieks	rotting rubbish	menacing shadows	starry sky	muffled sound

Character

2 Now describe a mysterious character that might appear in the street:

- How would they move? An old man shuffling furtively, limping, dragging one leg; a young boy scurrying; perhaps a young girl creeping nervously; a smart lady striding purposefully?

- What might they be wearing? Long dark cloak and tall hat; barefoot and ragged clothes; a red silk scarf that stood out in the darkness?

- What are their actions? Waiting in the shadows, staring silently, peering in through the window; looking for someone; calling to someone; running away; nervous, angry, weary, cross ...?

For example:

Something moved. Or someone. A figure appeared in the darkness ...

Writing

Adding detail

Learning objectives

- Use more powerful verbs, e.g. *rushed* instead of *went*. (4PSV12)
- Look for alternatives for overused words and expressions. (4PSV14)
- Elaborate on basic information with some detail. (4Wf2)
- Choose and compare words to strengthen the impact of writing, including some powerful verbs. (4Wf7)
- Use a more specialised vocabulary to match the topic. (5Wn3)
- Develop some imaginative detail through careful use of vocabulary and style. (6Wf7)

Let's revise!

- Write the following sentence on the board:
  - The breeze was blowing through the trees.
- Ask the learners what we mean by adding detail, what details are and how we add details – by adding adjectives, adverbs, figurative language, facts, examples, and so on. Make a list of these on the board. Ask the learners to extend the sentence on the board, adding at least one detail, for example:
  - The warm breeze was blowing gently through the tall, towering trees.
- Begin a class list of powerful language – verbs, adverbs and adjectives – for future reference. Place this on the wall and encourage the learners to add to it when they discover something powerful in their reading books.
- Revise the importance of adding the appropriate amount of detail, whether it is in a fiction or a non-fiction text. Ask the learners to think of something they have read that included just the right amount of detail, which added to the usefulness or enjoyment of the text, for example: details of characters – how they spoke, moved, and so on; instructions – explaining that something should be done in a certain way to avoid a mistake.
- Ask the learners if they have ever read something that included too much detail, for example too much description that slowed the action up. Ask them to think of texts in which it would be inappropriate to have lots of descriptive language, for example instruction texts.
- Ask the learners to read Text A on photocopiable page 87 and discuss the issues with this text – too much detail, too much description, getting in the way of the facts.
- Ask them to rewrite the instructions so that they are more appropriate for their purpose.
- Read Text B together as a class. If the learners are unfamiliar with this traditional story, you could find versions in books or on the internet. Discuss what is wrong with this version, remembering that the purpose and audience of the story is to entertain children. Allow time for the learners to add appropriate detail to make the beginning of this children's story more entertaining.

Top tips

- It is important for the learners to realise that adding more detail to a text does not necessarily make it better! For example, long lists of adjectives can have the opposite effect – I went through the tall, towering, dark, misty, scary forest.
- Remind the learners that when writing stories, they should use a good balance of description, action and dialogue.

Study Guide

Pages 84–85 of the Study Guide contain more activities on adding appropriate amounts of detail.

Adding detail

A   How to eat a hard-boiled egg

1 First, using a long-handled, lightweight spoon, take the smooth, lightly speckled brown egg out of the boiling water, as it dances and bubbles in the crystal water of the shiny steel pan.

2 Next, taking care to manoeuvre the egg with precision, place the golden orb into a specially designed, brightly decorated egg cup.

What is wrong with this piece? Write the instructions in a clear and concise way.

1 _____

_____

2 _____

_____

B   'The Three Billy Goats Gruff'

There were three goats. One was big, one was middle-sized and one was small. They lived in a field near a river. There was a bridge over the river, but underneath the bridge lived a troll.

One day they wanted to cross the bridge to get to the grass on other side. The little goat tried to cross the bridge but the troll said, 'I'll eat you up!'

'Don't eat me,' said the little goat. 'Wait for my brother. He's much fatter than me!' So the troll let the little goat pass.

This version of the story is quite dull. Add some detail to the beginning of this story to make it entertaining for younger children.

_____

_____

_____

_____

_____

_____

_____

Writing

Organisation and paragraphing

Learning objectives

● Use paragraphs consistently to organise ideas, linking them using adverbials and sequencing them appropriately to support overall development of the text. (4Wf6, 5Wf6, 6Wf5)

● Use a wider range of connectives to clarify relationship ideas, e.g. *however, therefore, although*. (6GPw2)

● Use a range of devices to support cohesion within paragraphs. (6Wf6)

Let's revise!

- Begin by discussing the importance of text organisation, and in particular the use of paragraphs. Ask the learners, in pairs, to write down some rules about when you might use paragraphs in certain texts. For example, in:
  - **stories:** change of place, time, subject
  - **information texts** such as non-chronological reports to group similar information
  - **discussion texts:** to address each point (for and against).

- Revise the sequencing and linking of paragraphs. Explain how reference can be made to a previous paragraph through the use of an adverbial phrase or connective. For example:
  - **adverbial phrases:** the next morning, some time later
  - **connectives:** on the other hand, however, meanwhile.

- Remind the learners that in a good paragraph, all the ideas are linked, and one idea should lead to the next in an organised and orderly way, creating a sense of unity. Again this is often created by effective use of connectives. Model this by showing them the paragraph below:
  - The cheetah is the fastest land animal. Its powerful legs allow it to reach incredible speeds. However, these speeds can only be maintained over short distances. Therefore, a cheetah is a sprinter, not a marathon runner!

- Ask the learners to think of four facts about themselves and then write a paragraph in a similar way to the model above.

- Ask the learners to complete the practical activity on photocopiable page 89. Not only do they need to group the content of this fantasy text appropriately into paragraphs, but they need to organise the sentences within each paragraph, and then use the language to order the paragraphs. Discuss what helped them to complete this task.

Top tips

Create a list of useful connectives, adverbial phrases, and so on on a display or in individual learners' notebooks. Encourage the learners to use these in their writing and add to the list when they discover new words or phrases that may be useful in the future.

Study Guide

Pages 86–87 of the Study Guide contain further examples of text structure and organisation.

Organisation and paragraphing

1 Cut up the sentences below.

2 Sort the sentences into four piles:

- General introduction

- Knucker Dragon

- Frost Dragon

- Chinese Lung

3 Arrange the sentences in each pile to create four paragraphs that make sense.

4 Write out the passage, making sure the order of the paragraphs makes sense too.

Closer to home, the Knucker Dragon is found in damp woodland, preferring to be near rivers or ponds.	Interestingly, it is one of the few dragons that does not breathe fire, for obvious reasons.
Firstly, the most beautiful, the Frost Dragon, is usually found in cold climates.	Its horns, teeth and claws are used for defence against eagles and big cats.
It prefers to hide out in caves and rocky outcrops.	Many people do not believe in them.
An iceberg provides a perfect place for its lair.	Its beautiful shimmering red scales are usually only glimpsed from a distance.
There are many species of dragons in the world.	It is particularly fond of creatures such as rabbits, voles and rats.
In contrast, the exotic Chinese Lung is usually found in mountainous regions.	They migrate thousands of miles each year so that they can spend time in winter darkness.
It is known for its excellent camouflage.	It can sometimes be found hiding in abandoned igloos.
However, once you have seen one, you will be hooked. Here are three of my favourites.	It is not usually dangerous to humans, preferring to hide amongst the trees.

Writing

Audience and purpose

Learning objectives

- Show awareness of the reader by adopting an appropriate style or viewpoint. (4Wn2)
- Adapt the conventions of the text type for a particular purpose. (6Wn2)

Let's revise!

- Revise what is meant by audience and purpose:
  - **audience:** who you are writing for
  - **purpose:** why you are writing.
- Learners often forget these two important considerations, and just write to please the teacher or the marker. Ask the learners to think of reasons why it important to keep these two things in mind.
- Discuss how knowing the audience and purpose:
  - affects the style and tone of the writing
  - influences the choice of language and the level of detail
  - reminds the writer of the features that need to be included.
- Draw a table on the board using the headings shown below:

Text type	Examples of audience	Purpose	Examples of tasks
Persuasion	Parents, politicians, buyers	To persuade	Letter, flyer, advert

- List all the types of writing that the learners might be asked to do (persuasion; explanation; instructions; fiction story; newspaper-style reports; non-chronological reports; own versions of fables, myths and legends; letters; biography; autobiography) and discuss the audience and purpose for each.
- Point out that the purpose governs the features but it is the audience that often has the greatest effect on the content. For example, a story might be to entertain, but it will be a very different story if it is written for a five-year-old than if it is written for an adult.
- Ask the learners to complete photocopiable page 91 to revise the variations in style, vocabulary and layout linked to the audience and purpose of a piece of writing.

Top tips

When planning any writing activity always try to give the learners a specific audience and purpose. For example, you could ask them to write a set of instructions to give to the youngest children in the school to help them stay safe near busy roads.

Study Guide

Pages 88–89 of the Study Guide provide other opportunities to write for different audiences and purposes.

Audience and purpose

Read these simple sentences.

> I walked down the road. I was alone. The wind was blowing. It had started to snow. I felt very cold and tired. I looked behind me. I could see a shadow in the distance. I quickened my pace.

Now read this version, which is written as if the audience is the police and the purpose is to inform – to recount an incident.

> At 7.15 I was walking in a westerly direction along Juniper Road. I was alone at the time. It was a windy night and I noticed that it had begun to snow. I was feeling rather cold and tired as I had been working all day. It was as I turned the corner that I noticed a shadow behind me so I quickened my pace.

Now read this version, which is written as if the audience is a reader of a horror novel and the purpose is to entertain (or frighten).

> The wind was whistling around me as I turned into the long, dark alleyway. Cats crouched in the gutters, dustbin lids crashed into angry brick walls. I was exhausted and it had started to snow but I knew that I had to keep going. I couldn't stop now. Suddenly, I heard a scraping noise behind me! A silent shadow caught my eye. I quickened my pace.

1   What do you notice about the differences between the three pieces of writing, and how has the author achieved the differences?

_____

_____

2   Whether you are writing fiction or non-fiction, it is vital to keep both the audience and purpose in mind at all times. This should guide the style and content of your writing. Rewrite this same event for the following audiences and purposes:

   a   Audience: a five-year-old child; purpose: to entertain

   b   Audience: your secret diary; purpose: to recount.

Name: _____   Total: _____ /30

Quick quiz 4

1 Great story openings should:

- _____

- _____

- _____   [3]

2 Improve this opening paragraph for a time-travelling adventure story.

> It was a warm day. Matt was enjoying walking on the beach. The sea was beautiful. The gulls were noisy. There was a strange noise. Matt followed the sound. He found himself in a cave.

_____

_____

_____

_____

_____

_____

_____

_____

_____

_____   [7]

3 How could you end this story to link with the opening? Write a possible last paragraph.

_____

_____

_____

_____

_____

_____

_____

_____   [5]

Revise for Cambridge Primary Checkpoint English Teacher's Guide © Hodder & Stoughton Ltd 2013

Name: _____

4 Create a new character for a story set in your school. Someone new arrives –
is it a pupil or a teacher? Are they friendly or nasty? What special features
might they have? How do they speak, move, and so on? Give them a name.
Make your planning notes in the box below.

_____

_____

_____

_____

_____

_____

Write the opening paragraph, introducing the character to the reader.

_____

_____

_____

_____

_____

_____

_____

_____

_____

_____   [8]

5 What type of text is each of the following?

a The Boy Scouts' Handbook _____   [1]

b Book of Bedtime Stories _____   [1]

c Save the Tiger flyer _____   [1]

d Foxes – Friend or Foe? _____   [1]

e How to set up your machine _____   [1]

f My Holiday Diary _____   [1]

g The Life of Birds _____   [1]

Quick quiz 4 answers

1 Great story openings should:

For example:

- **introduce the setting**
- **set the scene**
- **introduce the character**
- **entertain**
- **hook the reader in**
- **make the reader want to read more**
- **establish the genre** [3]

2 Improve this opening paragraph for a time-travelling adventure story.

> It was a warm day. Matt was enjoying walking on the beach. The sea was beautiful. The gulls were noisy. There was a strange noise. Matt followed the sound. He found himself in a cave.

Look for:

- **description of the setting and the character – sea, waves crashing, sun glimmering**
- **appeal to the senses – sounds, smells, sand under his feet, and so on**
- **contrast – normal day – sudden change – discovery of cave – cold, dark, and so on**
- **cliff-hanger – what's going to happen next?** [7]

3 How could you end this story to link with the opening? Write a possible last paragraph.

For example:

- **back in the cave as if he'd never been away**
- **tell-tale mysterious signs – strange footprints, artefacts, ripped clothes**
- **walks out into the sunshine back on the beach** [5]

Revise for Cambridge Primary Checkpoint English Teacher's Guide © Hodder & Stoughton Ltd 2013

4 Create a new character for a story set in your school. Someone new arrives – is it a pupil or a teacher? Are they friendly or nasty? What special features might they have? How do they speak, move, and so on? Give them a name. Make your planning notes in the box below.

Write the opening paragraph, introducing the character to the reader.

Look for and comment on:

- **description that paints the character – little details**

- **sentence structure**

- **choice of vocabulary to create inference, adding to the depth of the character, for example how he speaks, moves, and so on**

- **use of figurative language – similes, and so on**   [8]

5 What type of text is each of the following?

a The Boy Scouts' Handbook **Information text – non-chronological report, instructions**   [1]

b Book of Bedtime Stories **Narrative**   [1]

c Save the Tiger flyer **Persuasion**   [1]

d Foxes – Friend or Foe? **Discussion**   [1]

e How to set up your machine **Instruction**   [1]

f My Holiday Diary **Autobiography – recount**   [1]

g The Life of Birds **Information – non-chronological report**   [1]

Name: _____

Practice test 1 (Non-fiction)

Section A: Reading

Spend 20 minutes on this section.

Read the text then answer the questions.

1   When was the first cartoon film made?

     ....   [1]

2   Who made *Gertie and the Dinosaur?*

     ....   [1]

Name: _____

3 Tick (✓) **two** boxes that give correct information about early cartoon making.

Inventors were fascinated by moving pictures in the nineteenth century. ☐

The first film was called *Gertie the Dinosaur*. ☐

Emile Cohl was American. ☐

Film makers wanted to bring pictures to life. ☐

They used film cameras to bring pictures to life. ☐   [2]

4 Summarise the main points of this article using about 30 words.

....

....

....

....

....   [2]

5 Tick (✓) the best description of the text. Tick **one** box.

It contains only facts. ☐

It contains mostly facts. ☐

It contains mostly opinions. ☐

It contains about half facts and half opinions. ☐   [1]

Name: _____

6 Compare these texts.

The information in both texts is the same but the style of language used is different.

Text 1	Text 2
The heavy workload of the illustrators was changed by the introduction of 'cel' animation. The drawings were put on clear sheets of film, called celluloid. One image could be put on top of another.	It was such hard work! The illustrators were really pleased when celluloid was discovered. This is a clear film and you could put the pictures on top of each other, a bit like tracing paper.

Tick (✓) the text you prefer to read.

Text 1 ☐   Text 2 ☐

Explain why you chose that text.

....

....   [1]

Read the following text, a report from Wikipedia, and then answer the questions.

How films are made

Film production occurs in three stages:

Pre-production – Preparations are made for the shoot, in which cast and film crew are hired, locations are selected, and sets are built. This is also the stage in which the ideas for the film are created, rights to books / plays are bought, etc.

Production – The filming is done and the raw elements for the finished film are recorded.

Post-production – The film is edited:

- production sound (dialogue) is concurrently (but separately) edited
- music tracks (and songs) are composed, performed and recorded, if a film is to have a score
- sound effects are designed and recorded
- any other computer-graphic 'visual' effects are digitally added
- all sound elements are mixed into 'stems' then the stems are mixed and married to the picture and the film is fully completed ('locked').

Name: _____

7 **(a)** What are the three stages of film-making called?

.... [1]

(b) Name three things that happen in the pre-production stage.

.... [1]

8 Tick (✓) **two** boxes to show which statements are FALSE.

Music is added at the time of filming. ☐

Rights to the book or the play have to be bought. ☐

When the film is completed it is locked. ☐

The actors have to build the set. ☐ [2]

9 Suggest a reason why pre-production is often considered to be the most important stage.

....

....

.... [1]

10 This question refers to both texts 'Cartoons' and 'How films are made'.

(a) What is the purpose of the subheadings in the text 'How films are made'?

....

....

.... [1]

(b) In the text 'Cartoons', four paragraphs are used.

Draw lines to link each paragraph with its main topic.

1st paragraph	Who were the first cartoon makers?
2nd paragraph	Why did cartoonists choose a simple comic style?
3rd paragraph	What is a cartoon?
4th paragraph	Why were cartoons first made?

[1]

Practice test 1 (Non-fiction)

Section B: Writing

Spend 25 minutes on this section.

11 The reading texts 'Cartoons' and 'How films are made' are both reports taken from information texts.

(a) Write your own non-chronological report for an information text about something that you know a lot about, but you know the reader doesn't.

For example:
- a sport or hobby
- a species of animal
- a place you have visited
- a special interest.

PLANNING:
Spend about 5 minutes making notes in this box.

Purpose and audience	[6] ☐	Punctuation	[2] ☐
Text structure	[5] ☐	Spelling	[2] ☐
Sentence structure	[5] ☐		

Name: _____

(b) Write your report here.

....

....

....

....

....

....

....

....

....

....

....

....

....

....

....

....

....

....

....

Practice test 1 (Non-fiction)

Section C: Grammar, punctuation and vocabulary

Spend 15 minutes on this section.

12 Which of the following word classes have been underlined in the sentences below: adverb, pronoun, noun, preposition?

<u>Inventors</u> of the nineteenth century were fascinated by moving pictures.	
The pictures flash by so <u>quickly</u>.	
Sound is edited <u>after</u> filming.	
<u>They</u> were pleased when celluloid was introduced.	

[2]

13 (a) Underline the main clause in this sentence.

> Fewer drawings were needed because of the invention of celluloid.

[1]

Using the information in the sentences below, make (b) a complex sentence and then (c) a compound sentence.

> Film makers were fascinated by moving images. They invented cartoons. It was early in the twentieth century.

(Remember to add the punctuation.)

(b) ....

.... [1]

(c) ....

.... [1]

Name: _____

14 (a) Change this sentence to the present tense.

Film makers first had to find a good story and a location, then they had to build a set.

....

.... [1]

(b) Change this sentence to direct speech.

The director told the sound man that the special effects could be added later.

....

.... [1]

(c) Change this sentence from active to passive.

The illustrator created some very lifelike cartoons of dinosaurs.

....

.... [1]

15 Correct two mistakes in this sentence. Do not change the meaning.

Emile Cohl maked the first cartoon film on 1908.

.... [1]

16 Choose a connective to make a compound sentence from these two sentences.

The location is very important for a film. The director must choose carefully.

....

.... [1]

17 Add three apostrophes to this sentence.

Im not sure if Ive seen McCays film. [1]

Name: _____

18 Add the missing punctuation to these sentences.

The film editor who was very experienced was not easy to work with.

....

.... [1]

How am I supposed to get this finished in time he yelled.

....

.... [1]

19 Change **three** of the underlined words in this sentence but keep the meaning the same.

<u>Many</u> people <u>still enjoy going to</u> the cinema to watch <u>films</u>.

....

.... [3]

Practice test 1 (Non-fiction) answers

Section A: Reading

Maximum mark: 15

Question	1		
Part	**Mark**	**Answer**	**Further information**
	1	1908	
Total	1		

Question	2		
Part	**Mark**	**Answer**	**Further information**
	1	Winsor McCay	
Total	1		

Question	3		
Part	**Mark**	**Answer**	**Further information**
	2	Inventors were fascinated by moving pictures in the nineteenth century. Film makers wanted to bring pictures to life.	
Total	2		

Question	4		
Part	**Mark**	**Answer**	**Further information**
	2	The summary must contain four points: reference to dates; early film makers; how cartoons are made; and the introduction of celluloid.	Award 2 marks for mentioning all four, 1 mark for two or three points, 0 marks for over 50 words.
Total	2		

Question	5		
Part	**Mark**	**Answer**	**Further information**
	1	It contains mostly facts.	
Total	1		

Question	6		
Part	**Mark**	**Answer**	**Further information**
	1	Compare these texts.	Only award a mark if the style or language is referred to, for example, formal / informal – do not accept just 'easier to read' or 'more interesting' on its own.
Total	1		

Question	7		
Part	**Mark**	**Answer**	**Further information**
(a)	1	Pre-production, production, post-production	
(b)	1	Three of the following – cast and film crew are hired; locations are selected; sets are built; ideas for the film are created; rights to books / plays are bought	
Total	2		

Question	8		
Part	Mark	Answer	Further information
	2	Music is added at the time of filming. The actors have to build the set.	
Total	2		

Question	9		
Part	Mark	Answer	Further information
	1	Award a mark if reference is made to preparation being important, or the need to have ideas, a set, actors, etc. before a film can be made.	
Total	1		

Question	10		
Part	Mark	Answer	Further information
(a)	1	Introduces the information; so you know where to find information; divides the information up; it is easier to see	
(b)	1	1st paragraph — Who were the first cartoon makers? 2nd paragraph — Why did cartoonists choose a simple comic style? 3rd paragraph — What is a cartoon? 4th paragraph — Why were cartoons first made?	Award 1 mark for all lines drawn correctly
Total	2		

Section B: Writing

Question 11

PURPOSE AND AUDIENCE	TEXT STRUCTURE	SENTENCE STRUCTURE	PUNCTUATION	SPELLING
Writing is well shaped and wholly appropriate to purpose. Clear viewpoint with a clear and consistent relationship between writer and reader is established and controlled. **6**				
The text type is used consistently, *e.g. features of non-chronological report are clear and appropriate to purpose.* Relevant ideas and content chosen to interest the reader, *e.g. details developed.* **5**	Well-crafted paragraphs contribute to control of text, *e.g. clear logical links between paragraphs.* **5**	Use of complex sentences is controlled including the position of clauses to focus attention. Range of connectives may be developed, *e.g. 'although', 'meanwhile'.* **5**		
The text type is largely sustained, *e.g. features of information texts – non-chronological report.* The writer gives sufficient information for a reader to understand the content, *e.g. some detail with adverbials and expanded noun phrases.* **4**	Paragraphs are used to help structure the text and there may be evidence of appropriate links / subheadings between paragraphs. **4**	Some complex sentences are used to create effect, using expanded phrases to develop ideas, *e.g. noun, adverbial, adjectival and verb phrases.* A wider variety of connectives is used appropriately, *e.g. if, so, because, then.* Sentences are mostly grammatically correct. **4**		
Text type is used to convey writer's attitude to the chosen subject, *e.g. knowledge and enthusiasm for subject matter.* Some awareness of audience is shown. **3**	Paragraphs are sometimes used to sequence ideas. Balance of coverage of ideas is appropriate. **3**	Some complex sentences are used to extend meaning but not always successfully. Use of present tense is generally consistent. **3**		
General features of text type are evident, *e.g. information written on one subject; generally present tense.* Reader is given basic information, *e.g. relevant statements.* **2**	Some attempt is made to sequence ideas logically, *e.g. content clear for a biography.* Each section has an opening statement. **2**	Some variation in sentence openings is evident, *e.g. not always starting with noun or pronoun or other word.* Compound sentences are used but connectives are simple, *e.g. 'and', 'but', 'so'.* **2**	Sentences demarcated accurately throughout the text. Commas used in lists and to mark clause divisions. **2**	Correct spelling of common words with more than one syllable, including compound words. **2**
Some elements of the text type can be seen, *e.g. it is a non-chronological report.* **1**	Ideas grouped together although paragraphs may not be shown. **1**	Simple sentences are generally grammatically correct. 'and' may be used to connect clauses. **1**	Straightforward sentences usually demarcated accurately, *e.g. full stops, capital letters, question and exclamation marks.* **1**	Correct spelling of high frequency words. **1**

Award 0 when performance falls below lowest description.

Section C: Grammar, punctuation and vocabulary
Maximum mark: 16

Question	12		
Part	**Mark**	**Answer**	**Further information**
	2	Inventors of the nineteenth century were fascinated by moving pictures. — noun The pictures flash by so quickly. — adverb Sound is edited after filming. — preposition They were pleased when celluloid was introduced. — pronoun	
Total	**2**		

Question	13		
Part	**Mark**	**Answer**	**Further information**
(a)	1	Fewer drawings were needed because of the invention of celluloid.	
(b)	1	For example: Inventors, who were fascinated by moving images, invented cartoons in the nineteenth century.	Answer must include a subordinate clause.
(c)	1	For example: Inventors were fascinated by moving images in the nineteenth century so they invented cartoons.	Answer must have two equally weighted clauses joined by a connective.
Total	**3**		

Question	14		
Part	**Mark**	**Answer**	**Further information**
(a)	1	Film makers first have to find a good story and a location, then they have to build a set.	
(b)	1	'The special effects can be added later,' said the director to the sound man.	
(c)	1	Some very lifelike cartoons of dinosaurs were created by the illustrator.	
Total	**3**		

Question	15		
Part	**Mark**	**Answer**	**Further information**
	1	Emile Cohl made the first cartoon film in 1908.	
Total	**1**		

Question	16		
Part	**Mark**	**Answer**	**Further information**
	1	and, so, etc.	Award a mark for any connective that joins the two equal clauses.
Total	**1**		

Question	17		
Part	**Mark**	**Answer**	**Further information**
	1	I'm not sure if I've seen McCay's film.	Award 1 mark if all three apostrophes are in place.
Total	**1**		

Question	18		
Part	**Mark**	**Answer**	**Further information**
	1	The film editor, who was very experienced, was not easy to work with.	
	1	'How am I supposed to get this finished in time?' he yelled.	
Total	**2**		

Question	19		
Part	**Mark**	**Answer**	**Further information**
	3	For example: Lots of people continue to get pleasure from going to the cinema to watch movies.	Award a mark for every appropriate substitution.
Total	**3**		

Practice test 2 (Fiction)

Section A: Reading

Spend 30 minutes on this section.

Read this passage from *Running Wild* by Michael Morpurgo.

> I saw a shadow moving through the trees ahead of us. The shadow came into light, flickered into a flame of orange fire, and became a tiger. He came padding out of the forest onto the trail, stopped and turned to look up at us, hissing repeatedly, showing his teeth. Oona trumpeted again, and wheeled round to face him, trunk raised, ears displayed ...
>
> When the tiger began to circle us, Oona stood her ground and never moved a muscle. The tiger was right below me now, gazing up at me out of unblinking amber eyes, magnificent, awesome, terrifying. I went cold all over. I could hear my heart pounding in my ears. I could feel the hairs standing up on the back of my neck. I dared not breathe, but sat rigid on Oona's neck, clenching myself all over from my jaws to my fists, holding myself tight together, doing all I could not to betray my fear. I could smell the tiger's breath as he panted. I could see his pink lolling tongue. He was that close. One spring and I knew that would be the end of me, the tiger's twitching tail told me that it was very likely he was thinking the same thing.

1   Read these statements about the tiger. Tick (✓) **two** boxes that we know are TRUE from the passage.

He came padding out of the forest.   ☐

He was tall and thin.   ☐

He trumpeted.   ☐

He was hissing.   ☐

He was on fire.   ☐   [2]

2   What did the tiger look like as it first came out of the shadows?

....   [1]

3   What type of creature is Oona?

....   [1]

Name: _____

4   How do you know? Give evidence from the text.

.... [1]

5   How did the narrator feel as the tiger was circling him?

.... [1]

6   Why do you think the tiger was 'below' the narrator?

.... [1]

7   Read the description of the tiger's eyes. What does the author do and why?

....

....

.... [2]

8   Where do you think this story might be set? Give a reason.

....

.... [1]

9   How do you think the tiger was feeling? Find **two** statements that support
    your answer.

....

....

.... [2]

10 Do you think that the narrator was right to feel nervous? Give **two** reasons
    to support your answer.

....

....

.... [2]

Name: _____

11 Think of two similes Michael Morpurgo could have used to describe the tiger's eyes.

(a) ....

.... [1]

(b) ....

.... [1]

(c) How does a simile help the reader?

....

.... [1]

12 (a) The passage is a short extract from the book. From the evidence in this extract, which genre do you think the story is?

Tick (✓) the correct answer.

legend ☐

science fiction story ☐

historical story ☐

adventure story ☐

traditional tale ☐ [1]

(b) From whose point of view is the story written? Give a reason for your answer.

....

....

.... [2]

Name: _____

Practice test 2 (Fiction)

Section B: Writing
Spend 30 minutes on this section.

13 Read this story opening and imagine the scene.

> Jason sat up and opened his eyes. He felt dizzy.
>
> He looked around. Where was the tree-house? And his bike? And his rucksack full of goodies for the picnic?
>
> He'd arranged to meet Dan and Jodie in the woods behind his house. They'd made an amazing tree-house at the weekend and he remembered cycling along the path just a few moments ago, but now, everything had changed.
>
> The trees were taller. The ground was muddier. It was darker and creepier … and he was all alone.
>
> Just then he heard a sound …

- What was the noise?
- Where was Jason and how had he got there?
- Would he meet anyone?
- Would he ever find his way back?

Continue the story. Remember to include as much detail as you can.

PLANNING:
Spend up to five minutes making notes in this box to plan your story.

Revise for Cambridge Primary Checkpoint English Teacher's Guide © Hodder & Stoughton Ltd 2013

Name: _____

Write your story here.

....

....

....

....

....

....

....

....

....

....

....

....

....

....

....

....

....

....

....

....

Content and audience	[9] ☐	Punctuation	[4] ☐
Text structure	[5] ☐	Vocabulary	[3] ☐
Sentence structure	[5] ☐	Spelling	[4] ☐

Practice test 2 (Fiction) answers

Section A: Reading

Maximum mark: 20

Question	1		
Part	**Mark**	**Answer**	**Further information**
	2	He came padding out of the forest. He was hissing.	
Total	2		

Question	2		
Part	**Mark**	**Answer**	**Further information**
	1	A flame of orange fire	
Total	1		

Question	3		
Part	**Mark**	**Answer**	**Further information**
	1	An elephant	
Total	1		

Question	4		
Part	**Mark**	**Answer**	**Further information**
	1	Any of the following: Oona trumpeted, trunk raised, ears displayed	
Total	1		

Question	5		
Part	**Mark**	**Answer**	**Further information**
	1	Any words to describe absolutely petrified	
Total	1		

Question	6		
Part	**Mark**	**Answer**	**Further information**
	1	The narrator was sitting on the back of the elephant	
Total	1		

Question	7		
Part	**Mark**	**Answer**	**Further information**
	2	Anything to suggest that he makes them sound beautiful and terrifying at the same time – uses several strong adjectives – magnificent, awesome. The fact that they are unblinking means they are staring. Fixed on the narrator. Intimidating.	
Total	2		

Question	8		
Part	**Mark**	**Answer**	**Further information**
	1	For example: In a forest – moving through the trees; in India – that's where tigers and elephants are found.	
Total	1		

Question	9		
Part	**Mark**	**Answer**	**Further information**
	2	For example: Aggressive, angry, hungry, frightened, nervous, defensive, predatory – using appropriate statements from the text about hissing, showing its teeth, staring, circling, panting, twitching tail.	
Total	**2**		

Question	10		
Part	**Mark**	**Answer**	**Further information**
	2	Yes. For example: Tigers are dangerous animals, wild animals, tigers can kill you, he was alone, the tiger was very close, the tiger looked like it could spring at any moment.	
Total	**2**		

Question	11		
Part	**Mark**	**Answer**	**Further information**
(a) and (b)	2	For example: like two sparkling jewels	Any appropriate similes that pick up on the clues – amber, orange, unblinking, magnificent
(c)	1	Makes it easier to visualise, links with other experiences, paints a more vivid picture.	
Total	**3**		

Question	12		
Part	**Mark**	**Answer**	**Further information**
(a)	1	adventure story	
(b)	2	For example: It is written in the first person – I went cold all over	From the point of view of the person in the story – could be a boy, girl, man, woman
Total	**3**		

Section B: Writing

Question 13

CONTENT	AUDIENCE	TEXT STRUCTURE	SENTENCE STRUCTURE	PUNCTUATION	VOCABULARY	SPELLING
Imaginative detail is usually developed using a variety of techniques including imagery. During the course of the story, the development of the character/s is shown through actions and reactions. **5**		Paragraphs are used to structure the narrative. Dialogue is laid out correctly, with a new line for each speaker. **5**	Some complex sentences show control including the position of clauses to focus attention. Range of connectives may be developed, *e.g. 'although', 'meanwhile'.* **5**			
The character is well described with actions linked to key events. Suspense, or excitement, where used, is well built. **4**	A clear, consistent relationship between writer and reader is established and controlled. **4**	Paragraphs are used to help structure the narrative. There may be appropriate links between paragraphs. **4**	Some complex sentences are used to create effect, using expanded phrases to develop ideas, *e.g. noun, adverbial, adjectival and verb phrases.* A wider variety of connectives is used appropriately, *e.g. 'if', 'when', 'because'.* **4**	Punctuation is generally used accurately, including speech punctuation. Clauses are marked accurately by commas. **4**		Spelling is mostly accurate, including words with complex regular patterns. Allow plausible attempts at tricky polysyllables, *e.g. realised, interesting, wonderful, position, immediately.* **4**
Story is well crafted and focuses on either character or action. The story is concluded successfully and without rushing. Narrative viewpoint is established comfortably. **3**	The reader is engaged by the inclusion of appropriate detail. **3**	Paragraphs are sometimes used to sequence ideas. Ideas are organised simply with a fitting opening and closing that are mostly logical. **3**	Some complex sentences are used to extend meaning but not always successfully. Use of past and present tense is generally consistent. **3**	Commas are always used in lists and sometimes to mark clauses. Speech marks, if used, are accurately placed around words spoken, although other speech punctuation may not be accurate. **3**	Vocabulary is used effectively to create a strong image, *e.g. use of simile or metaphor.* **3**	Correct spelling of polysyllabic words that conform to a regular pattern is shown, *e.g. making, probably, clapped, possible, possibly.* **3**
The story is well placed in its setting. One event is described. **2**	Some attempt is made to engage the reader. The writer gives sufficient information for a reader to understand the contents / events described. **2**	Some attempt is made to sequence ideas logically, *e.g. content clear.* Openings and closings are sometimes evident. **2**	Some variation in sentence openings, *e.g. not always starting with the same noun or pronoun or other word.* Connectives are simple, *e.g. 'and', 'but', 'so'.* **2**	All sentences are nearly always demarcated accurately with full stops, capital letters, question and exclamation marks. Speech marks, if used, may not be accurate. **2**	Some evidence of accurate vocabulary choices. **2**	Correct spelling of common words with more than one syllable, including compound words. **2**
The story has a simple plot (in the context of the given prompt). **1**	The reader is given basic information that is relevant to the narrative. **1**	Story ideas are evident. **1**	Simple sentences are generally grammatically correct. 'and' may be used to connect clauses. **1**	Straightforward sentences are demarcated accurately, *e.g. full stops, capital letters, question and exclamation marks.* **1**	Simple, generally appropriate vocabulary is used – limited in range but relevant. **1**	Correct spelling of high frequency words. **1**

Study Guide activities answers

Phonics, spelling and vocabulary

Page 7 Have a go!

1 a rays **b** tow **c** beech **d** blew **e** try
2 a clock **b** fish **c** ditch **d** bridge **e** choir

Page 7 Writing and reading challenge

The moon was high in the sky. An owl hooted eerily somewhere in the distance. There was a smell of smoke and a strange crackling sound. Sam waited at the edge of the park. Should he go on or should he turn back?

Page 8 Have a go!

1 'dom' words: boredom, freedom, kingdom
'tion' words: examination, education, conversation
'ear' words: learn, search, early
'dge' words: hedge, ledge, wedge
'ch' words: choir, character, chemist
'au' words: pause, saucer, author

Page 9 Have a go!

2 a abundant **b** intelligent **c** extravagant **d** magnificent
e ignorant **f** violent **g** fragrant **h** evident
3 a evident **b** magnificent **c** abundant **d** intelligent
e extravagant **f** fragrant **g** ignorant **h** violent

Page 11 Have a go!

1 Any appropriate words, for example:
hard c: cup   soft c: peace   ck: back   k: king
2 a elastic **b** hectic **c** idiotic **d** plastic
3 a beautician **b** politician **c** magician **d** optician
4 a shriek **b** receive **c** priest **d** field **e** mischief
f piece **g** deceive **h** shield **i** relief **j** conceit
k yield **l** believe **m** receipt **n** grief **o** perceive

Page 11 Writing challenge

Any list of any *wa-* or *wo-* words, for example: water, work

Page 12 Have a go!

1 a view before **b** play again **c** not possible

Page 13 Have a go!

2 Any appropriate sentence to include the words plus the definition:
a *mid* means 'in the middle' **b** *anti* means 'against' or 'opposite' **c** *sub* means 'below'
3 Any appropriate root word with the suffix added correctly

Page 13 Writing challenge

Any examples of words where a root word has to be modified before the suffix can be added. This should be supported by a plausible rule, for example: When a word contains a short vowel phoneme followed by a single consonant, it is often necessary to double the consonant before adding the suffix – clap / clapping.

Page 14 Have a go!

1 Any appropriate choices for synonyms, for example:
a muttered, grumbled **b** cross, annoyed
c tranquil, relaxed **d** strolled, stormed
e grubby, muddy **f** sprang, bounded
g revolting, disgusting **h** soaking, drenched
i chilly, freezing **j** munch, devour

Page 15 Have a go!

2 Any appropriate antonyms, for example:
a high, raised up **b** ugly, unattractive
c untidily, messily **d** striding, marching
e noisily, thunderously

Page 15 Writing challenge

1 Rewritten using any appropriate synonyms, where the general meaning stays the same.
2 Using antonyms, the passage should have the opposite effect.

Page 16 Have a go!

1 a My eye-(sight) helps me to inspect the (site) of the building.
b The boy was delighted when he (won) more than (one) of the prizes.
c I wonder (who's) asking (whose) bike this is.
2 Any sentence that includes both homophones used appropriately (as question 1)

Page 17 Have a go!

3 a The mayor will <u>license</u> us to renew this <u>licence</u>.
b The baby started to <u>bawl</u> when he lost the <u>ball</u>.
c I will <u>write</u> the answer that is <u>right</u>. **d** I <u>passed</u> the bridge when I walked <u>past</u> the river. **e** As she <u>led</u> me down the path, I noticed the <u>lead</u> on the roof.
f Jill grew very <u>pale</u> when she picked up the heavy <u>pail</u> of water.

Page 17 Writing challenge

Any homophones with three spellings, for example:
to, two, too   there, their, they're   ewe, you, yew   doe, doh, dough

Any homophones with four spellings, for example:
awe, or, ore, oar   write, right, wright, rite

Page 18 Have a go!

1 a jellies **b** dishes **c** loaves **d** plates **e** glasses
f cloths **g** tables **h** shelves **i** coffees **j** cups
k keys **l** benches

Page 19 Have a go!

2 *-oes* endings: tomatoes, dominoes, cargoes, buffaloes, potatoes, mangoes
-os endings: pianos, radios, videos, patios, discos, photos, stereos, studios

Page 19 Writing challenge

Any words with irregular plurals, for example:
woman, women   goose, geese   tooth, teeth

Grammar and punctuation

Page 22 Have a go!

1 **a** herd **b** swarm **c** pack **d** collection **e** flock
  f litter **g** shoal **h** fleet
2 **a** string **b** band **c** bundle **d** bunch **e** bouquet
  f herd **g** crowd **h** pride

Page 22 Writing challenge

Any appropriate ideas, for example: a dazzle of sunflowers

Page 23 Have a go!

1 Masculine: husband, uncle, bull, prince.
  Feminine: niece, nun, bride, lioness.
  Common: pupil, guest, traveller, doctor, friend, patient.
  Neuter: fork, camera, hotel, car.

Page 23 Reading challenge

Discuss which pronouns occurred most often and revisit which of these determine possession

Page 24 Have a go!

1 **a** Draw **b** Give **c** rub, try **d** Colour **e** Cut
  f Go **g** Join **h** Hang

Page 25 Have a go!

3 **a** is sown, harvested **b** are separated **c** are ground
  d is transported **e** is used **f** is sold
4 **b** We separate the seeds from the ears of corn.
  c We grind the seeds to make flour.
  d Lorries transport the flour to the bakery.
  e The bakers then use the flour to bake bread.
  f Bakeries and supermarkets sell the bread to us.

Page 25 Writing challenge

2 Separate the seeds from the ears of corn.
3 Grind the seeds to make flour.
4 Transport the flour to the bakery.
5 Use the flour to bake bread.
6 Sell the bread through bakeries and supermarkets.

Page 26 Have a go!

1 **a** sharply (*m*) **b** yesterday (*t*) **c** there (*p*)
  d seldom (*t*) **e** around (*p*) **f** badly (*m*)
  g tomorrow (*t*) **h** everywhere (*p*)

Page 27 Have a go!

2 Any appropriate sentences; possible combinations
  include:
  fight heroically   arrive punctually   wait patiently
  speak fluently   promise faithfully
3 Root adjective: tall, wide, dry, sharp, wet, happy.
  Comparative adjective: taller, wider, drier, sharper,
  wetter, happier.
  Superlative adjective: tallest, widest, driest, sharpest,
  wettest, happiest.

Page 27 Writing and reading challenge

1 **a** worse – worst **b** no comparative or superlative
  (it's either private or it isn't) **c** further – furthest
  d more – most
2 For example: entire   fatal   final   half   main

Page 28 Have a go!

1 **a** at **b** in **c** across **d** behind **e** through
  f over **g** under **h** during
2 Any appropriate preposition or prepositional phrase
  used only once, for example:
  a between **b** past **c** into **d** behind

Page 29 Have a go!

3 Any appropriate sentences, for example:
  a I couldn't solve the puzzle so I had to give up.
  b I said I would look after my sister. **c** The bright
  colour was going to stand out. **d** I find it hard to get
  up in the morning. **e** We had run out of petrol.
  f The teacher said he would look into the problem.
  g Although I was tired, I wasn't going to give in.
  h I didn't expect to run into you here.

Page 29 Writing challenge

Any appropriate prepositions to make the day sound less
dangerous, for example:
It was a windy day and a branch of a tree fell <u>past</u> the
man's head. He decided to move, so he walked quickly
<u>across</u> the busy road and sat down <u>on</u> a park bench. Just
at that moment a rabbit ran <u>in front of</u> him. He followed
it <u>through</u> the trees but he soon got tired so he sat down
and rested <u>by</u> the river. It was beginning to get dark and an
owl screeched loudly <u>near</u> his ear. He got up and headed
<u>towards</u> his home. He came to a sign that said 'Dangerous
Animals. No Entry!' He turned and there, standing <u>far
away from</u> him, was an enormous lion.

Page 30 Have a go!

1 **a** subject: The boy; verb: walked **b** subject: The
  children; verb: entered **c** subject: Toby; verb: scored
  d subject: Sharks; verb: swim
2 **a** shone, blew; 2 **b** hunted; 1 **c** ate; 1 **d** started; 1
  e was, sold; 2

Page 31 Have a go!

3 Any appropriate sentences using a connective to join
  the clauses, for example:
  a The sun was very hot so I went home. **b** The boy ran
  across the road but the man stood still. **c** The meal
  was disgusting and I felt sick. **d** The train was full so
  everyone complained. **e** The ball went through the
  window and there was a terrible noise.

Page 31 Writing challenge

Passage rewritten using any appropriate connectives,
for example:
I wanted to go to the park <u>but</u> it was cold, <u>so</u> I put on
a coat. I asked my brother if he wanted to come. We
went outside and we started to walk down the road. The
pavement was icy <u>and</u> I nearly fell over. We arrived at the
park <u>but</u> my brother ran on ahead. He ran towards the
river <u>so</u> I shouted at him. He did not stop. He jumped <u>and</u>
he landed on a thick layer of ice. He slipped <u>and</u> fell over.
It looked so funny <u>but</u> I told him off. It was a dangerous
thing to do <u>as</u> he could have gone through the ice into the
cold water.

Page 33 Have a go!

Any appropriate complex sentence, for example:

1 Although it was rickety and old, the fence stayed up in
  the high wind.

  The fence, even though it was rickety and old, stayed up
  in the high wind.

  The fence, despite being rickety and old, stayed up in
  the high wind.
2 Suki and Suraj got full marks in the test because they
  had worked hard.

  After having worked hard, Suki and Suraj got full marks
  in the test.

  Suki and Suraj, as soon as they had worked hard, got full
  marks in the test.

3 As the man had sold all his vegetables, he packed up the stall.

The man packed up the stall when he had sold all his vegetables.

The man, because he had sold all his vegetables, packed up the stall.

Ensure pronouns are used where appropriate.

Page 33 Writing challenge

Any appropriate sentences containing conditional clauses

Page 35 Have a go!

1 Mrs Grisly, the scariest teacher in the school, stormed into the classroom.
2 She was a mean-looking individual, with a small, beaky nose.
3 She wore a grey suit, flat shoes, thick stockings and a small pair of glasses on the end of her nose.
4 Menacingly, she glared at the children in front of her.
5 Only the brave, and that was not very many of them, dared to meet her gaze.
6 However, even the brave ones soon began to tremble and look away.

Page 35 Writing challenge

Personal choice; focus on the use of commas within sentences

Page 36 Have a go!

1 Longer form: the cave belonging to the dragons, the saddles belonging to the horses, the car belonging to the man, the eggs belonging to the birds, the computer belonging to the teacher, the surgery belonging to the doctors, the car park belonging to the shops, the mane belonging to the zebra, the kitbags belonging to the footballers.
Shorter form using an apostrophe: the dragons' cave, the horses' saddles, the man's car, the birds' eggs, the teacher's computer, the doctors' surgery, the shops' car park, the zebra's mane, the footballers' kitbags.

Page 37 Have a go!

2 James' mouse was always escaping! He would jump over the fence into Mr Jones' garden, sneak past Old Sally's kitchen window and nip through Mr Patel's gate. He always forgot to shut it! As soon as he was free, the mouse would head for James' school. He would run through the teachers' car park, creep inside the school's front door and make straight for James' classroom. Luckily, James' teacher always laughed and said, 'Isn't it lovely to see someone so keen to come to school!'

Page 37 Writing challenge

A list of as many contractions as possible and what they are short for, for example: don't – do not; won't – will not

Page 38 Have a go!

Direct speech – for example:
Jamelia called out to Amina, 'Hey, I want to show you something!'
'What is it?' asked Amina.
'I'm not telling you,' replied Jamelia. 'It's a secret.'
'Where is it then?' asked Amina.
'Back home,' said Jamelia. 'Come round and I'll show you.'

Reported speech – for example:
Jamelia called to Amina that she wanted to show her something. Amina asked what it was, but Jamelia would not tell her. Amina then asked where it was. Jamelia replied that it was at her house. She invited Amina round so that she could show it to her.

Page 39 Writing challenge

Personal choice, focusing on using reported speech; for example:
You'll never guess what happened today. Miss Trunchbull had a real go at this boy called Nigel. Her body and face seemed to swell up. She said that he was nothing but a piece of filth and asked him if his father was a sewage-worker! …

Page 41 Have a go!

Personal choice – any sentences showing appropriate use of punctuation as used in the examples on page 40 of the Study Guide

Page 41 Writing challenge

Personal choice – a short advertisement (like the one on page 40 of the Study Guide) using many different forms of punctuation appropriately, with correct meaning

Reading

Page 45 Have a go!

1 In Holland, many centuries ago.
2 The best tulips were worth thousands of guilders and he wanted to win the biggest award of the year.
3 Two from: She lit an oil lamp. It would not be common to go to lace-making classes today. The food is cooked in a pot over the fire.
4 The wife had skinned it, chopped it up and put it in the stew because it was getting dark and she thought it was an onion.
5 The merchant was probably very cross with his wife and extremely upset about his prize bulb.

Page 45 Writing challenge

Diary entry, using: first person; past tense; informal style; events described in chronological order; some empathy with the character; extra details added for effect; some historical reference. For example:

A terrible thing happened today. I had been so busy since daybreak, scrubbing the sheets in the wash tub, cleaning the scullery and sweeping the yard. Suddenly I noticed the time and realised that I should be getting ready to leave for my weekly lace-making class. My husband always looks forward to a good meal waiting for him when he returns from work, so I rushed around and made a delicious vegetable stew. I remember thinking at the time that one of the onions was particularly large and juicy. I left the pot simmering over the fire and hurried along to my class.

When I returned, I found my husband pacing the floor in a terrible rage. When I asked him what was wrong, he slumped down into his old armchair and sobbed. I didn't know what to do to console him. Eventually he told me that I had chopped up his prize tulip bulb and put it in the stew. I think it was the worst moment of my life. I sat down and sobbed with him.

Page 47 Have a go!

1 It contains some very strange creatures that are definitely not real.
2 Rebecca was frightened – her finger was shaking as she pointed.
3 gleaming like a headlight of a motor-bike
4 The Swardlewardles did not even notice the sharp thorns.
5 A mouth that had so many teeth it resembled the keyboard of a piano.

Page 47 Reading challenge

1 & 2 The drawings should reflect the information given in the passage.
3 Good descriptions help to bring the settings or characters to life, and similes help the reader to visualise the content of the text by likening it to something that may already be known.

Page 49 Have a go!

1 Mat and Martha
2 a gentle voice that the children enjoyed listening to
3 to entertain the children but also to pass on traditional stories; to explain difficult things in life – historical events, people's actions
4 men from another continent
5 angry, sad
6 Personal choice with a reason for the choice

Page 51 Have a go!

1 six
2 one – that we know of

3 present – as if it is happening now – a commentary
4 Clarice Bean's – the narrator's
5 She doesn't really like them – they annoy her
6 objects, rubbish, anything she has in her room
7 It draws the reader in – allows them to empathise with Clarice
8 Three from: Family disagreements, relationships, brothers, younger brothers sharing rooms, old age – Grandad cannot hear, overcrowding in the house, moods, arguments

Page 51 Writing challenge

Personal choice, maintaining the viewpoint

Page 52 Have a go!

1 A fable – the characters are talking animals and it has a moral at the end

Page 53 Have a go!

2 The lioness
3 They all have different characters so that each cub can react differently to the situation and a moral can be drawn from the outcome.
4 Any plausible moral that fits with the story, for example:
   a If you rush in without thinking you might make the situation worse.
   b If you shy away from a situation you will never achieve anything.

Page 53 Reading and writing challenge

2 Any appropriate story following the original model

Page 55 Have a go!

1 Any two examples from the poem, such as:
   The willow is like an etching, / Fine-lined against the sky
   The willow's music is like a soprano, / Delicate and thin
   The willow is sleek as a velvet-nosed calf
2 Two of the following:
   The ginkgo is like a crude sketch, / Hardly worthy to be signed.
   The ginkgo's tune is like a chorus / With everyone joining in.
   The ginkgo is leathery as an old bull.
   The ginkgo's like stubby rough wool.
   The gingko forces its way through grey concrete; / Like a city child
3 One of the following: Wherever it grows, there is green and gold and fair.   Protected and precious   Somehow it survives
4 The city sky is cold, harsh and grey, like metal.
5 The poet is captivated by the beauty of the willow and enjoys looking at its delicate form – it is 'like an etching' with 'fine lines' and 'streaming hair'. However, she has a deep love and respect for the ginkgo, although it is not very beautiful, because it has to struggle to survive – 'my heart goes to the ginkgo'.

Page 55 Reading and writing challenge

2 Any example of two contrasting places, animals or objects described using a range of similes

Page 57 Have a go!

1 Early one morning; outside the front door of a house, in a dusty deserted road
2 Two
3 Accept answers that show that Abbi is worried about something and in a hurry, for example: She 'seems flustered and is looking anxiously all around'. 'You've got to come quickly.' 'Something terrible has happened.' She is 'looking panic stricken'. She 'begins to run down the path.'

4 She wants to tell her mum where she is going.

5 Three of the following: stage directions   characters' names in margin   new line for every speaker   split into scenes   no speech marks

Page 57 Reading and writing challenge

2 Accept any eight-line exchange between Jamelia and her mother, set out correctly, for example:

Jamelia: (*walking quickly back into the kitchen*) Mum – I've got to go out. I won't be long.

Mother: What do you mean, you've got to go out? You haven't had your breakfast yet.

Jamelia: I'll have something later. Abbi's waiting.
(*Jamelia starts to walk towards the front door*)

Mother: Well bring her in for a minute while you have something to eat.

and so on

Page 59 Have a go!

1 She rescued it from the empty lot on the corner.

2 No – it wasn't in working order. It had missing wheels, a broken axle, a ripped seat and missing panels.

3 It had to be pushed and dragged back home.

4 No – she wasn't. She took one look at it, raised her one eyebrow and asked why Benita had dragged the old wreck home.

5 It is a recount. It is informal, in the first person and past tense. It shows viewpoint. The events are retold in chronological order.

Page 59 Reading and writing challenge

2 Any recount of a childhood memory, demonstrating first person, past tense and chronological order

Page 61 Have a go!

1 Two

2 Teachers

3 Yes – she attended two art schools

4 She ran her own company making exotic chandeliers and lampshades.

5 Other people's conversations, seeing something funny happen

6 Third person, past tense

7 It would be in the first person.

Page 61 Reading and writing challenge

2 Personal response, in correct style

Page 63 Have a go!

1 There is a direct appeal, making the reader feel he or she has been singled out above thousands of young hopefuls – YOU have been chosen!

2 It has a double meaning. It could be referring to being out in space, or to something that is absolutely amazing.

3 Two from: alliteration – Vantage Vacations, Venturing aboard the Venus Voyager   slogan – Don't Delay – Apply Today   humour – Your friends will never have seen holiday photos like these!   powerful language – offer of a lifetime, greatly reduced price

4 Personal comment, drawing on the features of persuasive text

Page 63 Reading and writing challenge

2 A personal persuasive piece – must include as many of the persuasive features as possible to create a really effective text

Page 65 Have a go!

1 Which are better: books or films?

2 The author wanted to find out what happened in her book

3 Build up a thousand pictures in her head

4 On the other hand

5 The pictures on the screen didn't match the pictures in her head

6 To make it more exciting for the film

7 Personal response

8 Personal response, indicating differing viewpoints

Page 65 Reading and writing challenge

2 Personal response, using correct style and language features

Page 67 Have a go!

1 rules

2 A magnifying glass

3 Top left – it starts with going on a bug hunt

4 get down; move; keep; steady

5 Number the rules

Page 67 Reading and writing challenge

2 Personal response – appropriate style, language and layout

Page 69 Have a go!

1 25 years

2 Provides time for rest and dreaming

3 Rapid eye movement

4 During REM sleep, about five times in an eight-hour sleep

5 Present – it is explaining something that is continually happening

Page 69 Reading and writing challenge

2 Personal response, taking note of features, purpose and audience

Page 70 Have a go!

1 A mountain python

2 Instructions on how to corner the snake

Page 71 Have a go!

3 Frightened, because it was dangerous; possibly excited or curious, because it was something new and different

4 Personal response to describe a snake

5 Past – it is recounting something that has happened

6 Three from: first; early in the day; then; in the end

Page 71 Reading and writing challenge

2 Personal recount, demonstrating correct contrasting style and language features

Page 73 Have a go!

1 **a** sprints   **b** relay races   **c** middle- to long-distance running
The subheadings jump out at the reader, making it easy to find the information.

2 Oval

3 Usually 400 metres

4 An athlete who runs very quickly over short distances – 100, 200 or 400 m.

5 Jamaica

6 A marathon is run on roads as it is over 42 km and can take several hours to complete. It would be very boring to run round the track for this distance and it would mean nothing else could happen in the stadium for a considerable amount of time.

Page 73 Reading and writing challenge

2 Any information text about a sport or hobby, demonstrating correct use of paragraphs, headings and subheadings

Writing

Page 79 Have a go!

Personal response, based on the plan, using the traditional story as a model

Page 81 Have a go!

Personal response, demonstrating two contrasting openings and endings, based on previous story

Page 82 Have a go!

1 a Deep in a <u>dark</u> <u>black</u> space. <u>Dank</u> and <u>dark</u>, <u>bleak</u> and <u>black</u>. Is there any light at all? Yes, there's a <u>piercing</u> <u>white</u> light ahead: could it be the mouth of a cave, or the light at the end of the tunnel? It's a <u>tiny</u> relief compared with this <u>overwhelming</u> blackness, this <u>damp</u> <u>chilling</u> darkness, enveloping everything. What are the sounds? A drip of moisture from the roof, falling into a puddle in the <u>rough</u> ground underfoot. But otherwise there is just silence, leaving nothing to hear, as well as nothing to see. Where on earth am I?

b & c Personal response, focus on quality of description

Page 83 Have a go!

2 a Personal response, picking up on clues in the text, for example: appearance, unpleasant character – snapped, bellowed **b** Personal response, demonstrating contrast **c** Personal response, demonstrating points raised previously

Page 85 Have a go!

1 Personal response, demonstrating choices of appropriate amount of detail and description, for example:
Sita Achari walked through the familiar forest towards the old, dilapidated cottage where she had arranged to me her two best friends, Annie and Lou.

2 Personal response, demonstrating choices of appropriate amount of detail and description, for example: There are lots of amazing fish in the world. Some are enormous creatures, such as the …, found in …

Page 87 Have a go!

Explanation: The special feature of this kettle is that it has two chambers. The water is released from one chamber into the other by pressing a special valve at the top. One chamber is used to store the water. The other chamber heats the water.

Instructions:
A step-by-step guide
1 Put on your super spacesuit.
2 Climb into the pilot's seat.
3 Fasten your seat belt.
4 Put the spaceship into gear.
5 Count down and lift off!

Persuasive text: I want to write to you about the polar bears you keep in your zoo. I think it is important for them to live in their own habitat for a number of reasons. Firstly, it has been so hot this summer, they must really be suffering. They are suited to much colder climates. Secondly, they need to be active. They need to swim and catch fish from the sea.

Page 89 Have a go!

Personal response in letter form, demonstrating knowledge of purpose and audience

Page 89 Writing challenge

Personal response, demonstrating chosen format, purpose and audience

How much can you remember? Test 1 answers

Study Guide

See pages 20–21 of the Study Guide for the 'How much can you remember? Test 1' questions.

Maximum mark: 20

Question	1		
Part	**Mark**	**Answer**	**Further information**
(a)	1	table	
(b)	1	creep	
(c)	1	pipe	
(d)	1	moan	
Total	**4**		

Question	2		
Part	**Mark**	**Answer**	**Further information**
(a)	1	dge	
(b)	1	tch	
Total	**2**		

Question	3		
Part	**Mark**	**Answer**	**Further information**
(a)	1	any word containing dge	
(b)	1	any word containing tch	
Total	**2**		

Question	4		
Part	**Mark**	**Answer**	**Further information**
(a)	1	century	
(b)	1	piece	
(c)	1	receive	
(d)	1	work	
Total	**4**		

Question	5		
Part	**Mark**	**Answer**	**Further information**
(a)	1	extravagant	
(b)	1	intelligent	
Total	**2**		

Question	6		
Part	**Mark**	**Answer**	**Further information**
	2	Synonyms: dismal, dingy, murky, gloomy Antonyms: bright, brilliant, dazzling, light	
Total	**2**		

Question	7		
Part	**Mark**	**Answer**	**Further information**
(a)	1	For example: *We wanted to sail around the island.*	
(b)	1	For example: *Sadly the island is not for sale.*	
Total	**2**		

Question	8		
Part	**Mark**	**Answer**	**Further information**
(a)	1	flies	
(b)	1	monkeys	
Total	**2**		

Study Guide

See pages 42–43 of the Study Guide for the 'How much can you remember? Test 2' questions.

Maximum mark: 20

Question	1		
Part	**Mark**	**Answer**	**Further information**
(a)	1	slippery	
(b)	1	quiet	
Total	2		

Question	2		
Part	**Mark**	**Answer**	**Further information**
(a)	1	The girl climbed the tree.	
(b)	1	The boy ate the apple.	
Total	2		

Question	3		
Part	**Mark**	**Answer**	**Further information**
(a)	1	(t)	
(b)	1	(p)	
Total	2		

Question	4		
Part	**Mark**	**Answer**	**Further information**
(a)	1	2	
(b)	1	1	
Total	2		

Question	5		
Part	**Mark**	**Answer**	**Further information**
(a)	1	For example: *Even though he had been up all night, the boy was not tired.*	
(b)	1	For example: *Although the wind was cold, the sun was shining.*	
Total	2		

Question	6		
Part	**Mark**	**Answer**	**Further information**
	10	'What have you got in your bag**?**' asked Simeon**.** 'Only a towel**,** some swimming shorts and my money**,**' replied Matt. They walked around the corner and froze**.** Unbelievably**,** there in front of them**,** stood a …	There are ten items of punctuation missing.
Total	10		

Study Guide

See pages 74–75 of the Study Guide for the 'How much can you remember? Test 3' questions.

Maximum mark: 20

Question	1		
Part	Mark	Answer	Further information
	1	Lynne Cherry	
Total	1		

Question	2		
Part	Mark	Answer	Further information
	1	Lynne Cherry	
Total	1		

Question	3		
Part	Mark	Answer	Further information
	1	She visited the Amazon rainforest to make sketches and get inspiration.	
Total	1		

Question	4		
Part	Mark	Answer	Further information
(a)	1	well-written	
(b)	1	beautifully illustrated gem	
Total	2		

Question	5		
Part	Mark	Answer	Further information
	1	Enjoyed by millions of children worldwide and translated into several languages	
Total	1		

Question	6		
Part	Mark	Answer	Further information
	1	He probably told the man how important the rainforest is to the environment. He may have said that it was also his home.	
Total	1		

Question	7		
Part	Mark	Answer	Further information
	1	When he looked around at all the creatures who rely on the forest, he considered the importance of this great, majestic tree and realised that it would be wrong to cut it down.	
Total	1		

Question	8		
Part	Mark	Answer	Further information
	1	The importance of the conservation of the rainforest and respect for all the creatures living there.	
Total	1		

Question	9		
Part	Mark	Answer	Further information
	1	Present tense	
Total	1		

How much can you remember? Test 3 answers

Question	10		
Part	**Mark**	**Answer**	**Further information**
(a) & (b)	2	Two from: Internet sites; magazines; newspapers; libraries; bookshops	
Total	2		

Question	11		
Part	**Mark**	**Answer**	**Further information**
	1	A review usually provides an independent opinion of the book and informs possible readers what to expect if they choose to read it. It may offer a summary or a taster and it may try to persuade customers to buy, or not to buy, the book.	
Total	1		

Question	12		
Part	**Mark**	**Answer**	**Further information**
	1	On the back cover	
Total	1		

Question	13		
Part	**Mark**	**Answer**	**Further information**
	1	To give a brief summary, enticing the reader to buy/ read the book. It does not give the ending away.	
Total	1		

Question	14		
Part	**Mark**	**Answer**	**Further information**
(a)	1	For example: The review is an opinion written by an independent reader; the blurb, by the publisher.	
(b)	1	For example: The review is much more detailed; the blurb is a very short summary.	
Total	2		

Question	15		
Part	**Mark**	**Answer**	**Further information**
(a), (b), (c)	3	Personal response, with valid reasons for choice	
Total	3		

How much can you remember? Test 4 answers

Study Guide

See pages 90–93 of the Study Guide for the 'How much can you remember? Test 4' questions.

Maximum mark: 42

Question	1		
Part	Mark	Answer	Further information
(a)	1	characters' names in margin; stage directions; no speech marks	
(b)	1	speech marks; uses words for said; new speaker, new line	
(c)	1	no speech marks; written in past tense; retells what has been said	
(d)	1	usually has characters and settings; usually written in chronological order	
(e)	1	written in chronological order; numbers or bullet points; imperative verbs	
(f)	1	persuasive language; appeals directly to the reader; may use questions	
(g)	1	past tense; recount of events; written in the first person	
(h)	1	past tense; recount of events; written in the third person	
(i)	1	written in the present tense; impersonal style; explains something	
(j)	1	past tense; usually answers the questions: Who? What? When? Why? Where?	
Total	10		

Question	2		
Part	Mark	Answer	Further information
	1	The time and place in which the story takes place	
Total	1		

Question	3		
Part	Mark	Answer	Further information
	1	Person, animal or creature involved in the story	
Total	1		

Question	4		
Part	Mark	Answer	Further information
	1	For example: when writing concisely, or giving instructions	
Total	1		

Question	5		
Part	Mark	Answer	Further information
	1	Several sentences that are grouped together, usually based around the same subject	
Total	1		

Question	6		
Part	Mark	Answer	Further information
	1	So that the style and content is appropriate	
Total	1		

Question	7		
Part	Mark	Answer	Further information
(a)	1	not true, imaginary	
(b)	1	true, based on fact	
Total	2		

Question	8		
Part	**Mark**	**Answer**	**Further information**
(a)	1	For example: *I saw Joe when I went to the shop.*	
(b)	1	For example: *I saw Joe after he had been on holiday.*	
Total	2		

Question	9		
Part	**Mark**	**Answer**	**Further information**
	1	Give 1 mark for naming a text and providing a suitable reason.	
Total	1		

Question	10		
Part	**Mark**	**Answer**	**Further information**
(a)	1	For example: *gnarled, ancient*	
(b)	1	For example: *twisting, gushing*	
(c)	1	For example: *pitch black, twinkling*	
(d)	1	For example: *immense, awe inspiring*	
(e)	1	For example: *delicious, mouth watering*	
Total	5		

Question	11		
Part	**Mark**	**Answer**	**Further information**
(a), (b), (c), (d), (e)	5	For example: *(a) The gnarled branches of the ancient tree snatched at the boy's clothing as he crept silently through the darkening forest.*	Accept appropriate answers following the example given.
Total	5		

Question	12		
Part	**Mark**	**Answer**	**Further information**
(a)	1	For example: *The crescent moon was casting mysterious shadows among the trees as the overgrown fronds began to shiver. Strange noises echoed eerily through the darkness and a nearby river splashed and fizzed over rocks as it met the sea.*	

(b)	1	For example: *'Don't go any further, Leon!' Louis whined from the edge of the forest.* *'Why not? It's fine. Don't be such a baby!' Leon replied, clambering over a fallen tree. 'What are you scared of?'* *'I'm not scared! It's getting late, that's all. We should be going back!'*	
(c)	1	For example: *Leon ignored the distant whine of his younger brother as he clambered over a fallen tree and headed deeper into the forest. Slipping and sliding on the uneven ground, he clung to trailing vines, beads of perspiration appearing on his brow. He knew his brother was right, he should go back, but there was something drawing him forward. He had to go on.*	
Total	3		

Question	13		
Part	**Mark**	**Answer**	**Further information**
(a), (b), (c)	3	For example: *(a) The creamiest chocolate – a smile in every bite*	Accept appropriate answers following the example given.
Total	3		

Question	14		
Part	**Mark**	**Answer**	**Further information**
(a)	1	For example: *snapped*	
(b)	1	For example: *stuttered*	
(c)	1	For example: *screamed*	
Total	3		

Question	15		
Part	**Mark**	**Answer**	**Further information**
(a)	1	For example: *stomped*	
(b)	1	For example: *sidled*	
(c)	1	For example: *stormed*	
Total	3		